The World-Famous
SAN DIEGO ZOO

By CLAUDIA PEARCE
Publications Department,
Zoological Society of San Diego

Photography by
RON GARRISON, KEN KELLEY,
F. D. SCHMIDT, AND DAVID GATLEY
Visual Services Department,
Zoological Society of San Diego
unless otherwise noted

Design by
WARNER DESIGN ASSOCIATES
San Diego, California

Printing by
ANDERSON LITHOGRAPH
Commerce, California

Copyright©2000 by the Zoological Society of San Diego, P.O. Box 120551, San Diego, CA 92112-0551. First Printing.
ISBN 0-911461-16-7 Library of Congress Card Number: 00-108002
www.sandiegozoo.org

Polar Bear
Plunge

Skyfari
West

Birds
of Prey

Ituri Forest

Albert's
Restaurant

Giant Panda
Research
Station

Wings of
Australasia

Bonobos

Gorilla
Tropics

Dog & Cat Canyon

Reptile
Mesa

Tiger
River

Owens
Rain Forest
Aviary

Scripps
Aviary

Heart of
the Zoo

Wegeforth
Bowl

Orangutans

Sun Bear
Forest

Elephant
Mesa

Fern
Canyon

Hummingbird
House

Flamingo
Lagoon

Bear Canyon

Kangaroo
Bus

Reptile
House

Children's Zoo

Skyfari
East

Exit

Entrance

Lory Loop

The World-Famous San Diego Zoo

 North

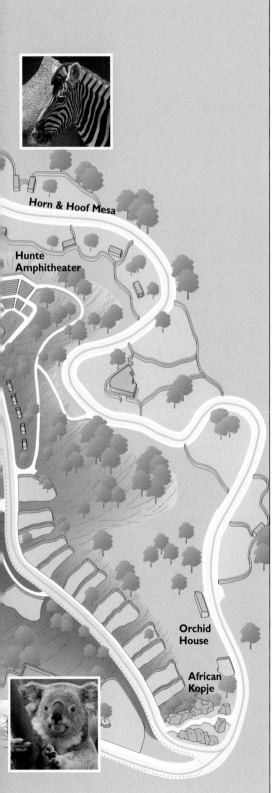

Horn & Hoof Mesa

Hunte
Amphitheater

Orchid
House

African
Kopje

Welcome to the World-Famous San Diego Zoo!

You are about to embark on a pictorial tour of the World-Famous San Diego Zoo. Before we set off on our exotic safari, however, a bit of background is in order. So we'll pause here for a brief overview of the Zoo, its history, and its vital role in the fight for the survival of many of the world's endangered species. And then, let the tour commence!

Visiting the World-Famous San Diego Zoo is a high point for everyone!

A World-Class Animal Collection With more than 4,500 mammals, birds, reptiles, and amphibians in its 100 lushly planted acres, the Zoo holds one of the finest animal collections in the world. More than three million visitors pass through our turnstiles each year to enjoy the incredible variety of exotic wildlife. When it comes to viewing the Zoo, you have numerous options—everything from guided bus tours, to a quick overlook via the "flying buckets" of Skyfari, to special educational tours that must be prebooked, to, of course, meandering down the paths on your own with the help of the map you receive at the entrance. And since walking and touring lead to hungry visitors, there are a variety of dining experiences available at the delis, cafes, and stands scattered throughout the grounds, as well as fine dining at Albert's Restaurant. We also have gift shops and stands featuring toys, books, games, souvenirs, and many hand-crafted artifacts from around the world. All of the profits from your purchases go back to support the work of the Zoo, which is operated by the not-for-profit Zoological Society of San Diego. The Society is dedicated to the conservation of endangered species and their habitats, and engages in conservation and research work around the globe. In addition to the Zoo, the Society also manages the 1,800-acre San Diego Wild Animal Park (more than half of which has been set aside as a protected native species habitat) and the Center for Reproduction of Endangered Species (CRES). You can find up-to-date information on the Society and its many programs at www.sandiegozoo.org or by calling (619) 231-1515.

Come for the animals, stay for the plants! And be sure to look up and out during your visit to see scenes such as this lovely view of Balboa Park's famous California tower framed by some of the Zoo's jacaranda trees.

And a World-Class Botanical Garden The San Diego Zoo is not only home for a world-class animal collection, it is also the home of a world-class botanical garden. There are approximately 700,000 plants on the grounds that create the lush, peaceful landscape the Zoo is known for. In addition to landscaping, the plants serve as the Zoo's major source for animal browse; they are an important research and educational resource for scientists and students from around the world; they provide shade for animals and visitors; and they are a crucial propagation source for nearly 100 endangered and threatened species and varieties. While the Zoo contains many different plant families, its American Association of Museums accredited collections include: Acacias, Bamboo, Cycads (primitive plants such as Sago palms), Palms, Erythrina (coral trees), Ficus (fig trees), Orchids, and Aloes. Other collections that were in the process of being documented for accreditation at press time: Trees (including Eucalyptus, Flowering Trees, and Tropical Hardwoods), Medicinal Plants, Zingiberaceae (gingers), Proteaceae (evergreen African shrubs), and Vines.

The founder:
Dr. Harry M. Wegeforth
on one of the Zoo's
first elephants.

Sheep and Goat Mountain: One of Wegeforth's first attempts to design more naturalistic enclosures.

How It All Began

The early history of the San Diego Zoo is both splendid and droll, much like its founder, Dr. Harry M. Wegeforth. Established in 1916, the Zoo was nothing like today's extensive, world-famous zoological garden. It began with a small collection of animals left over from San Diego's 1915–1916 Panama-California International Exposition in Balboa Park.

According to Wegeforth, who was an orthopedic surgeon, "On September 16, 1916, as I was returning to my office after performing an operation at the St. Joseph Hospital, I drove down Sixth Avenue and heard the roaring of the lions in the cages at the Exposition then being held in Balboa Park. I turned to my brother, Paul, who was riding with me, and said, "Wouldn't it be splendid if San Diego had a zoo! You know…I think I'll start one."

And so he did. He promptly spoke with the city editor at the *San Diego Union*, and the next day, the paper ran a story asking for volunteers to aid Drs. Harry and Paul Wegeforth in the creation of a local zoological society. Soon the two physicians had their board, as well as their lions, a "half-dozen moth-eaten monkeys, coyotes, and bears left over from the Exposition," and, within five years, much of their land. The Zoo was on its way.

A busy physician with his own medical practice, Wegeforth had tried hiring a string of men to direct the Zoo, including famed trapper, Frank "Bring 'em Back Alive" Buck. But few of them met his rigorous standards. Then he and his fellow board members suddenly realized that they had the ideal candidate right under their noses—Wegeforth's assistant, Belle Benchley. "Go ahead and run the place," they told her, "you're doing it anyway."

If it was Wegeforth who founded the Zoo, got it going, and established its animal-centric principles, it was Belle Benchley who helped it achieve national and even worldwide prominence. It was unheard of, in those times, for a woman to direct a Zoo. Even Benchley was surprised to find herself in the job.

"Even now," she wrote in her 1940 best-seller, *My Life in a Man-Made Jungle*, "I fail to recognize the steps leading to my advancement to the headship of the zoo staff, except that the zoo was poorly organized, and so, day by day, I was forced to assume added responsibility and to rely upon my own judgement." Benchley quickly graduated to doing basically everything: raising money, getting better deals on animal food, making sure there was enough in the accounts to pay the staff, answering questions from the public, dealing with keeper and animal problems, trading for new animals (under the tutelage of master-trader Wegeforth), handling the press, writing books, editing *ZOONOOZ*....The list went on and on.

Positively maternal when it came to "her" animals, Benchley often hand-raised young orphans like Mickey the tapir in her office. Furthermore, the intrepid director was often the one who rounded up animals that had gotten out of their enclosures. When a freak flood washed the Zoo's sea lions downtown, Benchley and a truck driver spent day and night recovering them all. And when a rattlesnake escaped, Benchley sneaked up behind the snake, which was as long as she was tall, grabbed it behind its head, and carried it upstairs to an enclosure. She and the board managed to keep the Zoo open and the animals fed during the Depression. And then, thanks to help from the Works Progress Administration (WPA), they were able to transform the Zoo with new buildings, plantings, and enclosure renovations.

When Benchley retired in December 1953, her hand-picked successor, Dr. Charles Schroeder, became director of the Zoo. The foresight of her choice would prove to be another tremendous boon for San Diego's beloved Zoo.

Wegeforth (saluting) on a Galápagos Islands collection expedition.

Benchley, then Director Emeritus, with Art Linkletter on his *House Party* show, live from the Zoo in 1958.

Always there for her animals: Benchley with a lion cub.

Don't Forget to Visit the
San Diego Wild Animal Park
**Just 30 miles northeast of
the Zoo, you'll find yourself
in the middle of the wilds of
Africa and Asia. At the San
Diego Wild Animal Park, you'll
see more than 3,000 animals
in naturalistic surroundings.
There, you can stroll through
the Heart of Africa, take the
Wgasa Bush Line Railway tour,
trek the Kilimanjaro Safari
Walk, and explore the exotic
gardens, shows, and exhibits of
Nairobi Village to see wildlife
like you've never seen it before.**

The Wild Animal Park is Born

By the 1940s conservation was already becoming an important issue. "The spread of civilization," Benchley had written, "has usurped gradually most of the proper places for animals to live, so that they have been forced into regions where they die for lack of proper living conditions. The best work in conservation is directly the result of the widespread interest in wildlife fostered by zoos." By the 1950s, with increased ease of travel and soaring human populations, the problem was even more serious. Dr. Schroeder had the vision to realize that there was a worldwide need for wild animal reserves, where borders between a zoo and the wild would blur. These reserves would not only serve as captive breeding grounds for zoo populations, but also as arks for endangered species. He resolved to start such a reserve in the sage scrub 30 miles northeast of the San Diego Zoo. On May 10, 1972, the San Diego Wild Animal Park opened its doors to the public. Visitors, rather than animals, would be enclosed in this new "zoo of the future," and would watch the vast herds of the plains from a silent monorail that circled the Park. Since its opening, the Park has been instrumental in breeding many endangered species, including rhinos, cheetahs, and condors.

**Founder of the Wild
Animal Park: Dr. Charles
Schroeder pounds in a
stake to designate where
the monorail track will
go (1970).**

9

There's nothing cute or cuddly about extinction. One of our most well-known research efforts is the study of giant pandas here and in China to learn about their breeding behavior and communication patterns. We also send $1 million a year to preserve the forests where giant pandas live. Protecting giant pandas in their native habitat doesn't just benefit these loveable animals. It also means a host of other endangered creatures— monal pheasants, golden monkeys, takins—and their entire ecosystem are being protected.

Leading the Fight for Survival

Today, the focus of many zoos has changed drastically, by necessity. No longer are they simply places of entertainment, where people can come to see and be amused by animals. As the world's human population skyrockets past 6 billion, forests are disappearing at alarming rates, thousands of plants and animal species are becoming extinct, and zoos have suddenly found themselves at the forefront of conservation efforts. Now, instead of making trips to the wild to capture species that are becoming increasingly rare, our curators and staff members make trips to the wild for conservation projects and research. The Zoological Society has become a world leader in the fight for the conservation and propagation of endangered species.

But when this shift of focus first began during Dr. Schroeder's era, many of the conservation and breeding techniques we take for granted today did not yet exist. As late as the 1970s and '80s, for example, there was no easy way to tell the sex of many birds and some reptiles. This was a big problem when keepers weren't sure if they had two males, two females, or one of each of the endangered animals they were trying to breed! Also, knowledge of animal reproductive cycles, nutritional needs, genetics, pregnancy diagnosis, viruses and parasites, and a whole host of other zoological data was limited at best.

In 1975, Dr. Kurt Benirschke, an acclaimed San Diego reproductive physician, spearheaded the establishment of a Society research and conservation branch: the Center for Reproduction of Endangered Species (CRES), complete with a "Frozen Zoo" consisting of a sperm bank and animal tissue samples. Thanks to the ongoing work of CRES, the field of animal reproduction has come an amazingly long way since then. Dr. Benirschke's Frozen Zoo has expanded to become an ark for the sperm, ova, and tissue/DNA samples of many of the world's endangered species. CRES workers have made numerous discoveries in the fields of animal husbandry and conservation. And it is now easier to sex many previously hard-to-sex animals through fecal analysis, ultrasound, and other methods. Today CRES is a world-class zoological research and conservation organization, with a top-notch staff of 80.

In 2000, under the leadership of its new director, Dr. Alan Dixson, a renowned zoologist and conservationist from Cambridge University, CRES established 12 post-doctoral fellowships for field conservation work. This new field work emphasis was critical. "If we don't act now," said Dr. Dixson, "we'll end up with signs by too many of our animals' enclosures that say: 'Extinct in wild, living only in captivity.' We don't want zoos to become living museums for animals that no longer exist in the wild."

Although Society curators, keepers, and researchers have long been involved in many conservation field work projects (the map on the following two pages gives only a partial list), their field work must necessarily be part-time, because of their jobs here in San Diego. The fellowships, on the other hand, are full-time positions that concentrate on especially critical areas of the world. The researchers are selected from the cream of the crop of the world's universities, based on factors that include their expertise in areas that complement the Society's goals and whether they live in the country of the projects. In this way, the Society hopes to make long-term commitments to its conservation work, complete with a local educational component.

CRES founder: Dr. Kurt Benirschke with his son Rolf at the Frozen Zoo.

A good example of how this new field emphasis is working is the Caribbean rock iguana project. Thanks to the work of CRES ecologist Dr. Allison Albert's, her staff, and the organizations they've partnered with, some of the most endangered lizards in the world—the eight species of Caribbean rock iguanas—are making a comeback. Because of human-introduced predators that eat the lizards' eggs and new hatchlings, several species of the iguanas now number less than a few hundred individuals. Using a highly successful technique called head-starting, the Society's conservation team rescues iguana eggs and brings them to protected sites where they raise the hatchlings until they are large enough to avoid becoming prey. Then they reintroduce them to the wild. The team has also placed iguana crossing signs at appropriate places on the roads, made school presentations that explain the iguanas' benefits to the Caribbean ecosystem, passed out iguana coloring books, and initiated other outreach efforts that help islanders value and better understand their largest native terrestrial animal. With such a strong Society outreach already in place, it only made sense to locate one of the fellowships in the Caribbean.

Glenn Gerber

Back from the brink of extinction thanks to a CRES headstarting program: an Anegada rock iguana.

Other areas where CRES hopes to add fellowships to support already-existing Society work are: China (pandas, golden monkeys, monal pheasants), Pacific islands (many endangered birds, Komodo dragons), Southern California (California condors, pronghorn antelopes, arroyo toads, bighorn sheep), Africa (black rhinos), and Latin America (Chacoan peccaries). Some of the Society's projects don't focus on a particular animal, they address a way of life. In Madagascar and Central America, for example, the Society has teamed up with other organizations to teach local people how to earn a living through butterfly farming and other methods that don't damage their forests.

NORTH AMERICA

Cheetah Captive Breeding,
Frozen Zoo, other CRES programs
Coast Horned Lizard,
San Diego County Native Birds,
Native Seed Bank,
Native Habitat Conservation
Bighorn Sheep

● Desert Tortoise

San Clemente Island ●
Loggerhead Shrike

● California Condor,
Pronghorn Antelope,
Arroyo Toad

● Mississippi Alligator
● Gopher Tortoise

● Hawaiian Forest Birds

● Thick-billed Parrots,
Monarch Butterfly
Conservation Project
Leatherback & Olive ●
Ridley Sea Turtles,
Baird's Tapir

● Caribbean Rock Iguanas
Hawksbill Turtles, Cuban Boa

● Harpy Eagle

● Giant River Otter,
Manatee, Harpy Eagle

● Andean Condors

Galápagos Tortoises ●

Peruvian Amazon ●
Conservation Project

SOUTH AMERICA

● Chacoan Peccary,
Habitat Conservation

There are only about 60
Micronesian kingfishers left
in the world. Thanks to the
Zoo's breeding program,
that number is growing.

Craig Racicot

An economical incentive
to preserve rain forests:
butterfly farming in
Central America.

The Society's *Proyecto Taguá* is
working to save Chacoan peccaries in their native range.

Our Work Around the World

Zoo staff members are notorious for taking busman's holidays—using their vacations to work on conservation field projects all over the globe. In addition to these informal projects, the Zoo, the Wild Animal Park, and CRES have many formal studies and projects, often in partnership with other organizations. The map you see above highlights many of the Society-sponsored projects.

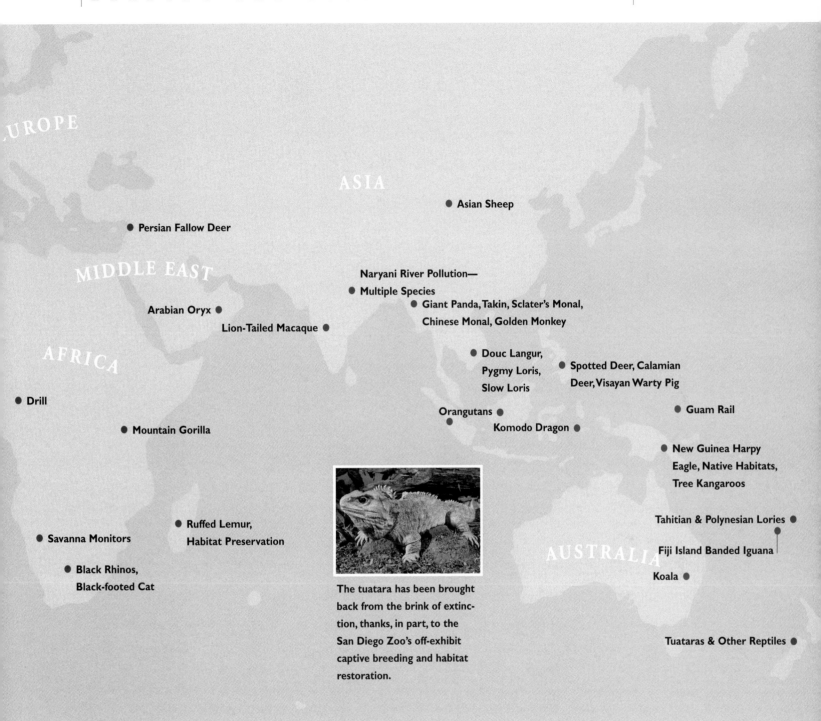

EUROPE

ASIA

● Asian Sheep

● Persian Fallow Deer

MIDDLE EAST

Naryani River Pollution—
● Multiple Species

Arabian Oryx ●

● Giant Panda, Takin, Sclater's Monal,
Chinese Monal, Golden Monkey

Lion-Tailed Macaque ●

AFRICA

● Douc Langur,
Pygmy Loris,
Slow Loris

● Spotted Deer, Calamian
Deer, Visayan Warty Pig

● Drill

Orangutans ●
●
Komodo Dragon ●

● Guam Rail

● Mountain Gorilla

● New Guinea Harpy
Eagle, Native Habitats,
Tree Kangaroos

● Ruffed Lemur,
Habitat Preservation

Tahitian & Polynesian Lories ●

AUSTRALIA

Fiji Island Banded Iguana

● Savanna Monitors

Koala ●

● Black Rhinos,
Black-footed Cat

The tuatara has been brought
back from the brink of extinction, thanks, in part, to the
San Diego Zoo's off-exhibit
captive breeding and habitat
restoration.

Tuataras & Other Reptiles ●

As you begin your pictorial tour in the next pages, you'll read about many more of the
fascinating endangered and threatened animals we are protecting here at the Zoo. You, as a guest at
the San Diego Zoo, help save animals too. Every dollar you spend enables us to continue our conservation work. And the more you experience the beauty and wonder of each of these unique plants
and animals, the more you can help us spread the word about working to protect them.

A Pictorial Tour of the World-Famous San Diego Zoo

Today's Zoo looks very different than the Zoo of Harry Wegeforth and Belle Benchley's day. Their successors have taken the founders' hopes for more spacious and natural habitats to levels the two could only have dreamed of, given the technologies available in their time. And the outstanding animal collection, overseen by Dr. James Dolan, Jr., Director of Collections, and Larry Killmar, General Curator, includes creatures that Wegeforth and Benchley didn't believe could successfully be raised in captivity. The newest exhibits create actual multi-species habitats that, as much as possible, mirror the animals' native lands with appropriate plants, terrain, sounds, and food and water sources. In many cases, the exhibits even approximate the area's climate through the use of refrigeration, heat, and/or mist systems. A walk through today's Zoo is a walk through the bioclimes of the world. Let's take a tour.

While it appears that flamingos have legs that bend backwards, that's not the case. It's just that their knees are up in their feathers. So they are actually standing on tip-toe, so to speak, and their ankles (which many people mistake for their knees) bend the same way ours do.

Birds of a Feather Flamingos are not only colorful and flamboyant, they also have fascinating behaviors that vary throughout the year. They are, in other words, the perfect sight to greet visitors as they enter the San Diego Zoo. Beginning in February, the Caribbean flamingos *Phoenicopterus r. ruber* can be seen courting en masse, with head flagging, wing salutes, squawking, and marching. By April, they begin nest building, and their island starts to look like a dirty lunar landscape with truncated, crater-like mounds going up everywhere. Carefully the sitting flamingos dribble mud in a circle around themselves to make their cozy nest mounds, taking breaks now and then to squabble and continue courting. By May, eggs begin appearing in the mud nests, and about a month later, the first chicks start hatching. Within five days, the chicks can swim and follow mom and dad to the beach. Then, the rest of the year, you can watch the flamingos care for their young as they pass through the white fluff phase, the awkward gray phase, and then to maturity in their second year. Although flamingos are not the most intelligent birds, working with them can be diverting. "There's a Zen to being with flamingos," says one of their keepers. "They all turn as one, like a big school of fish. They have a really strong flock mentality."

You can sometimes hear the capuchin bird *Perissocephalus tricolor* mooing, which is why it is also called a calfbird.

Bird Watching at the Bus Stop A guided bus tour is one of the best ways to get an overview of the Zoo. There are two options—the non-stop tour and the Kangaroo Tour. They both offer the same information, but the Kangaroo Tour stops at various locations, so you can hop out, walk around, and see animals such as gorillas and pandas that aren't visible from the bus, then hop back on the next bus to continue the tour where you left off. If you take the non-stop tour, be sure to look in the large aviary behind you on the boarding platform. There are all kinds of unique birds, including New Caledonian kagus and three birds from South America (pictured) which, at this printing, represent the only members of their species in North America.

New Caledonia's disappearing national bird: Unlike other flightless birds such as emus and ostriches, kagus *Rhynochetos jubatus* have large wings—they just don't use them. Instead, the two-foot-high birds forage on the forest floor, feeding on millipedes, beetles, snails, worms, and lizards. A kagu will stand motionless on one foot for long periods of time, watching and listening. Then, when a potential tasty morsel scurries by, the bird strikes with its long pointed beak. These good-looking, endangered natives of New Caledonia mate for life, which can be more than 20 years.

The long-wattled umbrellabird
Cephalopterus penduliger looks
like he's sporting a black necktie.

The mother of all thunbergias: If you stop for a
bite to eat in the Flamingo Cafe, check out the
vine with the impressive flowers you'll see on
your way in. Many of the *Thunbergia mysorensis*
in the continental United States sprang from
this modest vine!

The crimson fruitcrow *Haematoderus
militaris* isn't really a crow at all, but a
close relative of the umbrellabird.

Palm of plenty: Arenga palms such as the *Arenga engleri* by the second bridge in Fern Canyon are a common source of sugar in Southeast Asia. Sap from the palm's cut flower stalk is boiled down to make sugar, and fermented for alcoholic beverages. And the palm's water-resistant trunk fibers are used to make rope.

Hidden Passage to Paradise

Look carefully on the right side of Flamingo Lagoon and you'll see a shady path just under the bridge to the bus loading area. It leads to Fern Canyon, a peaceful refuge that's perfect for a meandering stroll. As you follow the pathway down, you'll be surrounded by lush green ferns of all sizes under a lacy canopy of purple-flowering jacarandas. Intertwined giant Burmese honeysuckle and Easter lily vines, Formosa palms, and other magnificent flora grow near the path and on the banks of the canyon's winding stream. Near the end of the pathway, you'll see one of the largest red ball trees *Dombeya cacuminum* in the continental United States.

The gold color on the edge of these red ball tree blossoms is actually pollen.

Flying Buckets

For a real overview of the Zoo, take the Skyfari. The "flying buckets" give a terrific bird's-eye view of the grounds, and they're a quick, fun way to get from the east end to the west end without a lot of hiking. In fact, if you want to see the polar bears first thing in the morning when they're most playful, hop into the Skyfari as soon as the Zoo opens. It lets you off right next to Polar Bear Plunge.

The Zoo's Signature Tree

You can see many members of the Zoo's striking coral tree collection throughout the grounds, and even surrounding the parking lot. What with all the different species, there's bound to be one coral tree or another in bloom practically all year around. Many are among the largest of their kind in the United States, including the *Erythrina lysistemon* (pictured) by the Skyfari's eastern terminal.

For the Young and the Young at Heart

You don't have to be a kid to enjoy the Children's Zoo. What with the pygmy marmosets that greet you as you walk in, the frisky otters, the fuzzy lesser panda, the prickly echidna, and the loveable wombat, there are more than enough super animals to keep humans of all ages fascinated. In addition to exotic animals, the Children's Zoo has many domestic favorites: mice that live in a bread house, placid bunnies, chinchillas, guinea pigs, miniature horses, pigs, and a Petting Paddock full of goats and sheep. Plus, several times during the day educators stroll around with a meerkat, a parrot, a rock hyrax, or some other cool animal that you can learn about up close. And don't forget to visit the compost station (complete with worm farm) on your way out!

The world's smallest monkey: South American pygmy marmosets *Cebuella pygmaea* only weigh four ounces and can easily fit in your hand. The cute little critters usually give birth to twins, and on rare occasions, triplets (above)!

There's more than one kind of panda in China: Like their bigger black-and-white neighbors, Chinese lesser pandas *Ailurus fulgens styani* are (a) incredibly adorable and (b) eat bamboo. Unlike giant pandas, however, these pandas are red, with long ringed tails, and they are related to raccoons.

Hard to swallow: Not surprisingly, when this echidna is threatened, it rolls up into a spiny ball—a time-proven method of discouraging predators. What you might not suspect is that the spiny anteater is also a good climber and can run swiftly when it wants to.

Reptile, Marsupial, or What? Found in Australia, Tasmania, and New Guinea, monotremes are a weirdly primitive order in the Animal Kingdom. They're not classified as reptiles, even though they lay eggs, have reptilian digestive, reproductive, and excretory systems, and have eye structures and certain bone structures like reptiles. Rather, they're classified as mammals because they are warm-blooded and nurse their young, but not as marsupials, even though they have cloacas and marsupial-like pelvic bones that can support pouches. Instead, monotremes have an order all to themselves that includes just two families: echidnas (spiny anteaters) like the Children's Zoo echidna *Tachyglossus a. aculeatus*, and duck-billed platypuses. While platypuses don't have an external pouch, echidnas do—the females put their eggs in their pouches and, after they hatch, keep their young there!

A warren of wombats: In the arid plains of central southern Australia, hairy-nosed wombats *Lasiorhinus latifrons* construct complex tunnel systems to link all their burrows together in mega-wombat-warrens. That way, the soft, furry marsupials can enter and leave any number of burrows to feed on grass and low shrubs.

Slipping, sliding, underwater somersaulting, and zooming through the water, these North American river otters *Lontra canadensis* have rapid metabolisms that give them boundless energy for playing and hunting in the wild. It also means they eat a lot. Every day their keeper gives each 15-pound otter 3 squids, a cup of cat chow, 2 or 3 trout, 3 smelts, a semi-cooked carrot, and a ball of Breeder's Choice Carnivore ground meat!

When predators threaten, Colombian brown spider monkeys *Ateles hybridus* have several options: They can flee through the treetops with the help of their prehensile tails, they can leap up to 32 feet to escape, or they can scare the predator away by breaking off a dead branch to drop on it, while barking like a terrier. Unfortunately none of these techniques works very well when the predator is a human. Because of their large size and noisy habits, these monkeys are easy to find, and they are avidly hunted for food.

Natives of the mountain rain forests of Papua New Guinea, Buerger's tree kangaroos *Dendrolagus goodfellowi buergersi* are able to hop from tree to tree, and they can jump 50 feet down to the ground without hurting themselves.

Brilliant bloomer: Animal close encounters, gatherings, and educational opportunities all happen under the bright blossoms and leafy branches of the Children Zoo's coral tree *Erythrina coralloides*.

Hide your maps and brochures before you go into the Petting Paddock; otherwise they might get eaten!

Don't Mess with the Queen! Eusocial animals live in multi-generational colonies where a single queen produces all the young with the help of a few breeding males, and the rest of the colony members serve as sterile helpers. Until recently, scientists thought that only insects like ants, bees, and termites were eusocial. Then in 1981, Jennifer Jarvis, a South African zoologist, electrified the zoological community with her discovery that the desert-dwelling, underground burrowers known as naked mole-rats *Heterocephalus glaber* were also essentially eusocial, living cooperatively in colonies of 45 to 300 individuals. How do you tell which mole-rat is the queen? She's the longest animal, and, though all the mole-rats care for her young and help feed them once they are weaned, she's the only one that suckles them. She's also the most aggressive, because she must fight off any females that are coming into estrus. At that point, the challenger female either gets so stressed that she becomes a "reproductively suppressed" follower, or she recruits a few males and moves off to start her own colony.

Making a Splash

While you're in the Children's Zoo vicinity, don't forget to make time for a sea lion show at Wegeforth Bowl. Its ever-popular flippered emcees are natural entertainers. You will not only come away laughing, but also come away with a better understanding of the natural behavior of California sea lions, owls, and other North American native creatures, as well as insight about what you can do to help preserve their habitats.

Seeing is believing: Animals like Akela the timber wolf are not just in the Wegeforth show for entertainment. When audience members get a chance to see how magnificent they really are, we hope they will be more likely to care whether or not the animals become extinct. Akela does just fine on stage, as long as her best friend Nala, a gregarious golden retriever mix, is around for moral support.

Truly regal: At first glance, you might mistake the Cuban royal palms *Roystonea regia* near Wegeforth Bowl for large concrete columns etched with horizontal segments. A quick look up, however, reveals that the columns are the trunks of huge and magnificent palms, and the rings are leaf-base scars.

Enchanted World

The Hummingbird House is a long-time favorite of Zoo visitors. Being in the aviary is almost like being in a fairy world, watching fantastic, colorful little creatures flitting by your face while surrounded by waterfalls and beautiful exotic plants. Besides watching the hummingbirds nest and feed, you may also see them bathe—they like to shower several times a day. Sometimes they sit in shallow water and splash, and other times they perch next to the falls and flap their wings and ruffle their feathers in the spray. You'll see more than hummers here. The aviary houses many of the Zoo's smallest and most delicate avian species, including the rare green pygmy goose *Nettapus pulchellus*, which isn't a goose at all, but a small "perching duck." One caution for those who want to visit: The aviary is closed to the public every year during the month of October.

Like all hummingbirds, these South American sparkling violetears *Colibri coruscans* not only drink nectar, but can also be seen "hawking" insects from mid-air.

San Diegans who grow nectar-producing plants or hang hummingbird feeders outside their windows are likely to attract Anna's hummingbirds *Calypte anna* like this one. There are about 328 species of hummingbirds in the New World, and thousands of plant species depend on them for pollination.

With its lime green head, turquoise breast, and other brilliant colors, there's no question why this gorgeous bird is called the paradise tanager *Tangara chilensis.*

If you look carefully, you're likely to see any number of carefully constructed nests in the aviary, such as the cup-shaped refuge of this oasis hummingbird *Rhodopis vesper tertia* from northern Peru. While most of the nests are rather small, the lesser green broadbills *Calyptomena viridis continentis* (far right) build long nests made of plant fibers and spider webs that are easy to spot—if you don't mistake them for a trail of debris.

Latin Romeos: South American white-bearded manakins
Manacus m. manacus **are often called the New World version
of birds of paradise. Just like some of their New Guinea
counterparts, the males carefully clear an "arena" for their
mating display, taking care to leave two small saplings standing
with their leaves stripped off. Then when a female happens
by, the manakin makes weird clicking and insect sounds, flaps
his wings, and projects his white throat feathers, all the while
dancing back and forth between each stick and his arena floor.
You can often see the Zoo's manakin displaying in his arena
near the Hummingbird House path just after the first bridge.**

It's All in the Cups When you're visiting the Hummingbird
House, don't forget to check out the nearby bromeliad garden.
The most well-known bromeliad is the pineapple, but there are
about 2,000 species of this rain forest plant—all of which are native
to the Americas except one African species. Most bromeliads collect
a pool of water in their centers and flower above the cup. Then
when insects and small animals stop by for a dip, or to eat the
microorganisms and larvae growing in the cup, the blossoms
also dip and pollination occurs. As you might guess, the water in
these cups can get quite fetid. While insects may not mind, Zoo
visitors do, so gardeners flush out the cups on a regular basis.

**Splendid relative of the pineapple:
the *Aechmea fasciata*.**

**An ecosystem in a bromeliad cup:
the *Neoregelia concentrica*.**

Experience the Wonders of an Asian Rain Forest

Embark on a jungle trek down a riverbed pathway that leads to a tiger's lair, a crocodilian pool, a fishing cat's den, and a marsh complete with cattails, fallen trees, and wafting mists. As you walk along the descending path, you'll be shaded by towering palms, coral and orchid trees, ferns, figs, bamboos, and gingers. It's Tiger River: Kroc Family Rain Forest, the Zoo's tropical rain forest bioclime. The exhibit was not only designed for the propagation of the approximately 100 rare animals that make Tiger River their home, but also to instill in its visitors a sense of wonder, discovery, and appreciation for the fragility of one of the world's most threatened environments.

Something to Sink Their Claws Into Tiger River's keepers do all they can to encourage tigers to use natural behaviors such as smelling and stalking to hunt for "prey." Instead of just feeding their charges in a dish, for example, while the tigers are in their bedrooms, keepers hide bones and ground meat all over the exhibit—in trees, in hanging burlap bags that must be "killed" to obtain the treat, and even frozen in ice! This excellent care, as well as the naturalistic environment, has not only produced contented cats, but also quite a number of offspring. After its great success breeding Sumatran tigers *Panthera tigris sumatrae*, the Zoo decided to concentrate on the even rarer Indochinese tigers *Panthera tigris corbetti*. At the time of this printing, this latest endeavor had resulted in three playful, bouncing Indochinese tiger cubs!

Paddybird: Unlike people who own fish ponds, rice farmers are happy to see herons wading in their paddies. That's because herons such as this Indian pond heron *Ardeola grayii* eat insects that damage rice. Like most herons, pond herons have specialized down feathers that never molt. Instead, the ends of the ever-growing feathers continually fray into a fine powder which the birds use to remove slime and oil from the rest of their feathers.

When this gorgeous young Indian pond heron is fully mature, its breast and head will be white.

Hope for this Toothsome Twosome Gharials *Gavialis gangeticus* have had a tough time of it in the last century: First people hunted them for their skins—to make shoes and luggage—and killed them because they were fish-catching competitors. Now, even though they are protected in their native range of India and the surrounding countries, the river-dwelling crocodilians are still having problems because of habitat destruction and accidental drowning in fishing nets. So every potential breeding pair of these highly endangered animals is important, including the Zoo's. The toothsome reptiles are called gharials because of a bowl-like protrusion at the end of mature males' noses called a *ghara*—Hindi for "pot." In 1999, the Zoo's male finally grew an adult-sized "pot." Here's hoping baby gavies will soon be making an appearance! (In transition: Soon the gharials will be moving. If you don't see them in Tiger River, look for them in their new larger enclosure on Reptile Mesa.)

Not the kind that bring babies: Complete with cattails, reeds, and fog, Tiger River's marsh aviary is home to more than a dozen species of rain forest birds, including these sociable milky storks *Mycteria cinerea*. These big white relatives of herons and spoonbills are in danger of becoming extinct because much of their habitat—Southeast Asian mangrove forests and marshland—has been cleared for agriculture. Fortunately, some of these marshlands are now protected.

Ready, set, pounce! While any cat worth its salt enjoys batting at swimming fish, Asian fishing cats *Prionailurus viverrinus* are specially equipped for fishing. Their partially webbed front paws enable them to swim up to a fish and bite it, as well as to sit by the side of a creek or swamp, scoop up unwary fish, and flip them on the bank for a quick meal. Another of the fishing felines' favorite techniques is to sit in the shallows and pounce on fish that swim by. The small cats also eat crustaceans, mollusks, frogs, snakes, birds, and small mammals.

Snout of Distinction While most people who see tapirs for the first time guess that they're related to elephants, pigs, or anteaters, the rotund, long-nosed animals are actually relatives of rhinos and horses. Since their eyesight is poor, tapirs compensate by using their noses for almost everything, including sniffing out food and predators, and as a snorkel when they're swimming or walking on a river bottom. Three of the world's tapir species can be found in Central and South America, and one—the Malayan tapir *Tapirus indicus* you see in Tiger River—is found in Asian jungles. The animal's unique black-and-white coloring helps it blend in with the dark and light patches in the dense rain forest.

Clumpers vs. runners: While the "running" bamboo varieties spread rapidly and are hard to get rid of, "clumping" varieties such as this *Bambusa vulgaris cv. Vittata* are easier to control and thus more often used in landscaping. In spite of its "vulgar" name, this large-diameter bamboo is quite attractive, and you can see it between the tigers and the tapirs in Tiger River. Other clumping bamboos are blessed with more flattering and exotic names, including Buddha's Belly, Fernleaf, and Golden Goddess.

Lizards don't consider them slow: Bengal slow lorises *Nycticebus coucang bengalensis* probably got named "slow" because of their leisurely locomotion. No swinging through the air with the greatest of ease for these primates. They traverse the treetops of Southeast Asian rain forests by progressing hand-over-hand and foot-over-foot. But that doesn't mean the wide-eyed primates can't move quickly on occasion. If they see something tasty, such as an insect, bird, or lizard, for example, they grip their branch with both feet (having opposable big toes makes this easy), and lunge forward to seize their prey with both hands.

These young lorises are both the same age, but one is a pygmy loris and one is a slow loris. Guess which is which!

In a class by themselves: Malayan lesser chevrotains *Tragulus javanicus ravus* are also known as mouse deer because of their small size—adults are no bigger than a large rabbit—and their secretive behavior. Chevrotains are one of the most primitive of the ruminants (cud-chewers), and have remained virtually unchanged for 30 million years. They evolved from a tusk-bearing mammal that was also the ancestor of giraffes, modern deer, and cattle. While these other animal groups eventually evolved protective head gear—antlers and horns—the chevrotains didn't. But they kept their tusks.

Better seen than heard: For such beautiful birds, Reinwardt's blue-tailed trogons *Harpactes r. reinwardtii* have a rather harsh-sounding call—it's penetrating, hoarse, and very distinct. The insectivores have two toes that point backwards to help them hang on to tree branches in the mountain forests of Sumatra and Java, where they make their home.

Crazy for Love Next door to the tigers is one of the most unique pheasants in the bird world—the great argus. Great argus pheasants *Argusianus argus argus* are named for the many-eyed watchman of Greek mythology because of the hundreds of three-dimensional-looking "eyes" on their feathers. The argus male has especially spectacular feathers, which can best be seen when he is in courtship mode. This happens fairly often during the breeding season since he spends most of his time trying to impress females. If he isn't preening his feathers, he's maintaining his display arena—clipping away overhanging branches, sweeping away plants and debris, and so on—so he has a smooth floor with plenty of room for his courtship dance. And periodically throughout the day, the argus announces his whereabouts to females and potential male competitors with loud two-note calls. Then when a female arrives, the real excitement begins. He begins dancing around her. At the dance's climax, he throws up his wings into two enormous half-circles around his head with hundreds of "eyes" that surround his real eyes, which, of course, are focused on her. At that point, the female either decides to move on, or sticks around long enough to mate before she leaves. And the male goes back to his courtship preparations in hopes of luring yet another female (or the same one) back to his dance floor. You can see the Zoo's argus pheasants in action from January through June—not only in Tiger River, but also in Parker Aviary (behind the siamangs) and Owens Rain Forest Aviary.

What happens to an argus male when an argus female walks by.

Wild and Wooly in Ituri Forest

Built in 1999, Ituri Forest is one of the Zoo's most entertaining places to watch inter-species interactions. Just past the okapis and hippos, you can see swamp monkeys play "grab-the-tail" with spotted-necked otters, groom them, and occasionally even hitch a quick ride on the otters' backs as they swim by! For their part, the otters climb low-lying trees and appear to enjoy monkeying around with their simian friends. An otter will roll over and bump a relaxing swamp monkey, for example. Then, when the monkey tries to grab its tail, the otter rolls quickly away, and then back again, as if tantalizing the monkey to catch it.

While most of the adult Schmidt's spot-nosed guenons stick with their own kind—swinging around in the trees high above the frolicking otters and swamp monkeys—their young enjoy mixing with the other animals. You can often see young guenons and swamp monkeys playing together.

Quick-fingered Allen's swamp monkeys *Allenopithecus nigroviridis* actually swim in rivers and catch fish with their hands in the wild—which probably explains why they're so good at playing "grab-the-tail" with the spotted-necked otters *Lutra maculicollis* in the Zoo.

Guenon's eye view of a forest buffalo: There's excitement among the forest buffalo *Syncerus caffer nanus.*
A new male has joined the females, and the keepers are hoping to see some mating activity soon. The
one-male-to-several-females ratio is natural for these buffalo. In Africa, young males that don't manage to
become the breeding male must head out on their own. And without the protection of the larger group,
they often fall prey to leopards or lions.

The real Ituri—an equatorial rain forest in the heart of the Democratic Republic of
Congo—is full of trees, brush, fallen logs, trip vines, and other dense and thorn-bearing vegetation,
not to mention 12-foot-long black mambas. Needless to say, it's a daunting place to navigate, even
with help from the short-statured Mbuti (Em-boo-tee) tribes who live there. A visit, however, does
have its rewards. The interior of the forest has breathtakingly beautiful vistas: colossal trees with
incredible buttressed roots, fantastical termite mounds that look like they belong in a J.R.R. Tolkien
landscape, huge flocks of iridescent butterflies, lush swamps, and more than 329 avian species. Plus
it has 52 mammal species, many of which are unique to the forest. Unfortunately, loggers, slash-and-
burn farmers, bushmeat hunters, and warring Congolese factions are making inroads into the Ituri,
and a number of its species are now endangered. So each new birth in the Zoo's Ituri Forest takes on
a poignant significance. If more is not done to protect the real Ituri, such zoo-born animals may
become the only members of their species left in the world.

Although he looks like an elderly gentleman, this Debrazza guenon *Cercopithecus neglectus* regularly performs 10-to-20-foot tree-swinging leaps that put circus acrobats to shame.

Velvet-skinned relatives of the giraffe, okapis *Okapia johnstoni* use their 18-inch prehensile tongues for all kinds of activities: stripping acacia leaves off a branch, for example, and wiping sleepers out of their eyes. But their tongues can't reach everywhere, so the fastidious animals enjoy having their ears cleaned on occasion—so much so that they lean into their keepers while it's being done.

Born August 31, 1999, Mashavu (which means "baby with chubby cheeks" in Swahili) stuck close to her mom at first. After all, she needed a boost to the water's surface in order to breathe. Now she's big enough to get breaths on her own. In five years, the outgoing river hippo *Hippopotamus amphibius* should be about the same size as her mom: 3,000 pounds—small potatoes compared to her dad, who weighs in at 5,000 pounds!

Like father, like daughter. Are they yawning, playing, threatening, or just saying "Ah"? Only the hippos know for sure.

Elusive Forest Dwellers

Most of the large spiral-horned antelopes graze in open habitats. The East African bongos *Tragelaphus eurycerus isaaci*, **however, are an exception. Though the shy, beautiful animals weigh about 500 pounds, they live in dense woodlands, where they are adept at remaining unseen in spite of their size.**

Fruit pulp, anyone? For several weeks before egg-laying, the monogamous great blue turaco *Corythaeola cristata* **regurgitates gifts of fruit pulp for his female. Then, once she lays the eggs, he and she share in their incubation. They also take turns with the brooding and feeding of their hatchlings.**

Congo peafowl *Afropavo congensis* like this hen are the only native African member of the pheasant family. All the other pheasant species live in Asia. How the Congo peafowl became isolated from their multitudinous Asian counterparts is a mystery that has yet to be solved.

Hogging the Attention

Whenever the red river hogs *Potamochoerus porcus* show off their latest litter, there's always an audience. The striped little piglets are fun to watch as they run and root, snorting and squealing, with pointy ears flapping. In addition to being good-looking, the intelligent pigs are extremely resourceful, which is probably why they're still alive in the wilds of Africa. Red River hogs are widely hunted because of their skill at sneaking into fields at night and rooting up crops in record time, as well as the fact that their flesh is said to be quite delicious.

A Place of Wonder and Tranquillity

If you need a peaceful, beautiful place to relax during your Zoo visit, head for one of the walk-through aviaries. A stroll through the Scripps Aviary gives you a feel of the avian life you'd see in an African forest—without the man-eating carnivores and poisonous snakes! The aviary even has gentle showers. So when you hear thunder, don't lean over the rail too far or you may get wet. Pause often during your stroll, and be sure to look up, as well as out and down. In the treetops, amid the storks, spoonbills, and ibises, you'll see large black birds whose bills look like giant pinchers. These African open-bill storks *Anastomus l. lamelligerus* are quite rare in captivity, and use their oddly shaped beaks to extract snails and other fresh-water mollusks from their shells. Also, flitting among the trees, you're likely to see a golden-breasted starling *Cosmopsarus regius magnificus*—one of Africa's most colorful and dazzling birds. Swimming in the pools, you'll see African pygmy geese *Nettapus auritus*, which are actually relatives of teals and ducks and just happen to have a goose-like bill. And near the bottom of the aviary, protected in special enclosures because they're so rare, you'll see black-casqued hornbills *Ceratogymna atrata* (below) and the unique southern purple-crested turaco *Tauraco p. porphyreolophus*, with its purple crest, blue forehead, red eye circles, green neck, and bright under-wings that flash red when it flies. With its wealth of beautiful plants and brilliant birds, the Scripps Aviary is the perfect place to sit quietly, watch, and listen.

To eat a snail, this open-bill stork first pins down the mollusk with its upper bill and uses the sharp tip of its lower bill to cut the muscle that attaches the snail to its shell. Then it deftly extracts its meal, usually leaving the shell unbroken.

Turacos eat mostly fruit, including berries that are extremely poisonous for humans. Like most turacos, this southern purple-crested turaco has red pigment in its wing feathers called turacin that comes from the copper in its diet. The turacin is responsible for the dramatic red flash you see when the African birds are flying.

My what big feet you have! Like its parents, this young African jacana *Actophilornis africana* has extra-long toes that enable it to walk on lily pads and other water plants.

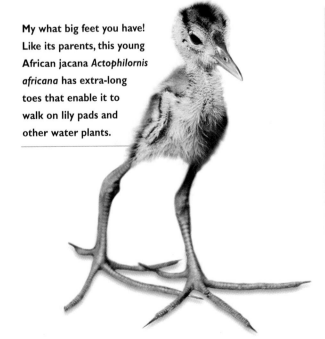

Africa's forests are rich in bird life—ibises, spoonbills, rollers, pygmy geese, and this dazzling golden-breasted starling, which is getting ready to jump into the pool of a waterfall.

Gentle Giants

After leaving the upper reaches of Scripps Aviary, continue your African rain forest walk in Gorilla Tropics next door. The exhibit is home for a troop of western lowland gorillas *Gorilla g. gorilla*, as well as bonobos (pygmy chimps), Angolan colobus monkeys, and even more African birds and plants.

Godmother: Because Alvila had not had an infant since 1986, the aging gorilla ranked fairly low in the troop hierarchy. But when Alvila became a surrogate mom for the hand-reared Imani, her status suddenly rose. Memba, the head silverback, decided she was now worthy of his attention. To everyone's surprise, Alvila became pregnant and had a daughter. Keepers named the unexpected bundle of joy Azizi—Swahili for "rare treasure."

A Family in Danger A large silverback (the gorilla alpha male) can be quite intimidating to meet in the wild, especially if he thinks you might be dangerous. To frighten enemies, the 6-foot-tall muscular male stands up, beats his chest, roars, and runs around pulling up vegetation. These intimidation techniques were one of the reasons Westerners used to think gorillas were ferocious man-eaters. (Movies like *King Kong* didn't help matters.) In fact, gorillas are actually vegetarians. They have strong family bonds, and, except when threatened, are usually peaceful and even shy. Unfortunately, threats to these gentle giants are accelerating. And it's not just because of habitat loss.

African tribes have long hunted monkeys and apes to supplement their diets with "bushmeat." But it used to be just subsistence hunting. Now, however, because of the high prices ape flesh commands on the market, bushmeat has become a commercial industry. The situation is exacerbated by overpopulation, logging, and wars that drive Africans to encroach deeper and deeper into previously pristine habitats. If the present accelerating rates of slaughter continue (with 3,000 to 6,000 gorillas "harvested" each year, along with tens of thousands of monkeys and apes—including bonobos), gorillas and bonobos could become extinct in the wild by the end of this decade. All that will be left is the troops living in zoos. This tragedy is especially horrendous for those who realize how closely we are related to the great apes. Gorillas share more than 97 percent of their DNA with us, and bonobos even more.

Peaceable Primates More than 98 percent of the bonobo's DNA is identical to ours. So it's not surprising that bonobos *Pan paniscus* (also called pygmy chimps) have a lot in common with us. While their arms are long and agile, and they are covered with glossy, black fur, their eyes appear as soulful as any human's. Furthermore, their kids play some of the same games that our kids do. You can observe young Zoo bonobos playing King of the Mountain—where one chimp parades around on top of a hill or rock, while the rest try to pull him or her off—and Blind Man's Bluff—where young chimps with their hands over their eyes run around chasing each other. And you can watch adult bonobos playing with their young, socializing, and using hand-made tools. You might, for example, see one of them stripping the leaves off a branch in order to dip it into a honey-filled hole to get a treat. One characteristic bonobos are especially known for is their ability to get along. Like all higher primates, bonobos occasionally have tiffs with each other. But unlike humans and chimps, they have never been observed killing one of their own kind.

Simian Transformers

Eastern Angolan colobus monkeys *Colobus angolensis palliatus* **transform rather drastically between birth and maturity. Newborns are born with curly, pure-white fur, but by about three or four months of age, the monkeys have gained their adult coat—straight black fur with a striking white fringe. The agile African leaf and fruit eaters were named for the Greek word** *kolobus,* **which means mutilated or docked, because of their lack of an opposable thumb. This unique feature enables them to swing through the treetops more easily.**

Raptor!

In the wilds of South Africa, crowned eagles *Stephanoaetus coronatus* **catch monkeys and antelopes that weigh as much or more than themselves. They dive down on their victims and strike with their talons, often with so much force that their prey is killed instantly. Needless to say, if there were not a fence separating the Zoo's colobus monkeys from the pair of crowned eagles next door, the monkeys would end up as dinner for the eagles, as their wild counterparts often do. Like most raptors, the male crowned eagle is smaller than the female. It is thought that his smaller size makes it easier for him to catch many different kinds of prey when he's feeding his mate as she incubates their eggs. The Zoo's pair have chosen a nesting spot that the public can see, and they raise a chick there almost every year.**

Almost Holy

One of the main reasons the world's top bird people make pilgrimages to the San Diego Zoo is the Wings of Australasia. The exhibit has so many of nature's rarest and most fantastic bird species that ornithologists would have to spend a lifetime traveling to the far reaches of the globe in hopes of seeing all of them in the wild—and even then they might not succeed. That's because many of the birds are endangered, and some, like the Micronesian kingfisher, are even extinct in the wild. Which is why our bird curator prefers to give these particular species extra protection in Wings of Australasia's state-of-the-art enclosures, rather than housing them in the walk-through aviaries.

While the Zoo has almost 500 species of birds (the largest collection in the U.S.), it specializes in lories, hornbills, pheasants, and birds of paradise. Parrot people travel to San Diego just to see our lories and parrots, and pheasant people come for the pheasant collection. Together, the Zoo and the Wild Animal Park have the most varied collection of hornbills in the United States, and have probably hatched more young hornbills than any other collection in the world. The Zoo is also one of the world's most successful breeders of birds of paradise. So when you walk into Wings of Australasia, enter with awe. You are seeing an avian preserve unlike any other.

Safe haven for lories: They've been called "dapper little lovebirds in blue-and-white tuxedos," and when you see them, you can't help falling in love with Tahitian blue lories *Vini peruviana* (above). So it comes as a shock to realize that, unlike the peach-faced lovebirds you buy in pet shops, these sociable little nectar-eaters are threatened. Other extremely rare lories in the exhibit include Fiji's collared lories *Phigys solitarius* (right) and Tonga's blue crowned lories *Vini australis*. Thanks to their comfortable surroundings and their conscientious keepers, most of these rare birds are breeding. While much of the Zoo's world-class lory collection can be found in Wings of Australasia, you can see more of the South Pacific birds (as well as the colorful Edward's fig parrot *Psittaculirostris edwardsii*, above right) in Lory Loop—the path behind the tour bus entrance on the way to the koalas.

Vulture or parrot? The Pesquet's parrots *Psittrichas fulgidus* of New Guinea look like a cross between a vulture and a parrot, which is probably why they are called vulturine parrots. The Zoo's pair of Pesquet's is one of the only captive breeding pairs in the world.

The rarest bird at the zoo: The beautiful Micronesian kingfisher *Halcyon c. cinnamomina* is extinct in the wild, and there are only about 60 birds in eight institutions, worldwide—all of which reside in the U.S. Although the Zoo has successfully bred these kingfishers, it can't reintroduce them to Guam, their native habitat. That's because brown tree snakes (believed to have stowed away aboard military aircraft) now thrive in Guam's forests. Their fondness for eggs and chicks has meant the annihilation of many of the island's avian species, including this kingfisher.

Kenneth Fink

One of a kind: The horned parakeet *Eunymphicus c. cornutus* is the only parrot in the world with feathers that resemble horns, and it's found only in New Caledonia.

Getting ready for the "walling in:" A rhinoceros hornbill feeds his mate so she'll know he can provide for her when she's walled in.

We Tried to Tell Them There Were No Tree Snakes, but They Wouldn't Listen!
Like all hornbills, this rare southern Sulawesi hornbill *Penelopides exarhatus sanfordi* (above) has ultra-protective nesting habits that you can see from February through May at the Zoo. Once the female hornbill has found a tree hollow big enough to suit her, she and the male begin patching any unwanted crevices or holes with mud, food, saliva, and droppings. Then the female enters the nest and helps the male wall her in except for a small hole, so no predators like monkeys or tree snakes can get her or her eggs. The male then feeds her through the nest hole while she incubates the eggs and cares for the new hatchlings. Since the female is walled in for almost four months, she and the chicks also use the nest hole to eject their droppings. When the chicks are old enough, the female breaks out of the nest, and the cycle starts again the next breeding season. Even the rarest hornbills in the Zoo—the white-headed hornbills *Aceros l.leucocephalus*— are breeding successfully in Wings of Australasia. You can see more hornbills north of the pandas in Dog and Cat Canyon, including the Javan rhinoceros hornbill *Buceros rhinoceros silvestris* and Asia's great hornbill *Buceros bicornis.*

No wonder their parents want to protect them! Young hornbill chicks.

The most spectacular knobs:
You can see red-knobbed hornbills
Aceros cassidix in Parker Aviary,
behind the siamangs. Below, top
to bottom: white-headed, West
African long-tailed, and rhinoceros
hornbills.

Who's the Number One Romeo? When it comes to courtship in the bird world, there are many virtuosos. While it's easy to pick out top contenders for Number One Romeo, however, it's almost impossible to decide who's the best of the best. The tragopans, with their suddenly-engorging bright horns and wattles are certainly contenders. So is the Bulwer's wattled pheasant (left), with its flapping, fleshy blue wattles and magnificent white-fanned tail. But what about the argus—calling, dancing, and spreading his huge wings of "eyes" in his specially constructed arena? Or, for that matter, his more common counterpart, the peacock? And then there are New Guinea's bizarre and beautiful birds of paradise. The mature males in these 40-odd species have such extravagant, varied adornments, that it's hard to believe they're related to each other. They've got plumes, frills, capes, special tail and wing feathers, and quills that they flaunt in any number of fantastic dance moves to attract females. You can see several species of the birds in Wings of Australasia, as well as in the bird of paradise enclosures north of the upper reaches of the Skyfari's west terminal. As for who's the Number One Romeo—we can't make up our minds. You'll just have to visit during mating season (February through mid-June), check out all the birds' courtship displays, and decide for yourself.

Salvadori's birds of paradise *Paradisaea raggiana salvadorii* call, dance, flail their feathers in weird contortions, and work themselves into a frenzy to impress females.

This male superb bird of paradise *Lophorina superba feminina* is not courting at the moment. But when he does, he fluffs his black neck feathers into a huge cowl that makes him look like a grotesque hooded phantom. This, apparently, makes him irresistible to female superbs.

Magnificent birds of paradise *Diphyllodes magnificus hunsteini* quiver their curlicue tail feathers to entice their females.

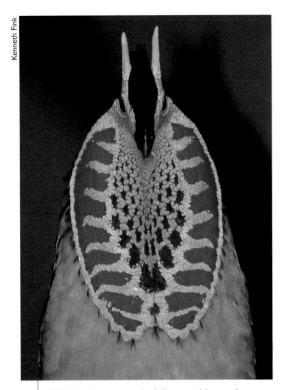

Kenneth Fink

A Cabot's tragopan in full courtship mode.

Simply Shocking!

How do you win the heart of a female Temminck's tragopan? Apparently, by popping out from behind a rock and scaring her. For this reason, the Zoo has obligingly placed rocks for Temminck's *Tragopan temminckii* males to hide behind in their enclosures so they can pop out and startle the females. During mating season (January through May), you'll know the male tragopan is ready to display if you hear him making a series of loud double clicks. Stick around, and you'll see him pop up like a Jack-in-the-box, with his colorful engorged wattle and "horns." You can see Temminck's, as well as Cabot's tragopans *Tragopan caboti* behind Polar Bear Plunge to the south.

Our Bird Curator's Favorite Birds

Usually, male tragopans like this endangered Blyth's tragopan *Tragopan b. blythii* look like unassuming colorful pheasants. But you should see them when they're courting! All of a sudden multi-colored "horns" stick up from their heads and an equally spectacular "bib" or wattle engorges below their beaks and across their breasts while they stand upright with their wings spread. Also known as horned pheasants, tragopans are one of the few pheasants that spend more time in trees than on the ground. All five of the rare tragopan species live in the cloud forests of Asia.

K. Fink & D. Rimlinger

It all happens in a few seconds: the display progression of a Temminck's tragopan.

In Transition!

A guidebook for the San Diego Zoo can never be completely up-to-date, because the Zoo's exhibits are always being upgraded. At press time, the historical exhibits of Bird & Primate Mesa were still standing. By the time you read this, they may be in the process of being torn down to make way for more naturalistic and spacious enclosures for our new Heart of the Zoo exhibits. So if you don't find your favorite monkeys, honey badgers, and pacaranas on your visit this time, come back next year and see them in their new homes!

Honey Badger

Vernay's ratels *Mellivora capensis vernayi* are pretty much left alone in nature because of their formidable defense mechanisms. They have skin so thick that it can resist a bee's sting, porcupine quills, and even dog bites. Plus their leathery hide is extremely loose. So if a predator grabs a mouthful, ratels can easily stretch around and bite and claw their foe. Also, ratels can secrete an extremely vile-smelling solution from their anal glands. Needless to say, the animals have no natural predators. They will even waltz right up to a bee hive and break in to secure their favorite food (hence their other name—honey badgers). If all this is true, why are they disappearing from the wild? It's the usual story. Ever-growing human populations are destroying their habitat, so they can't get the mammals, birds, eggs, reptiles, berries, and honey they need to survive.

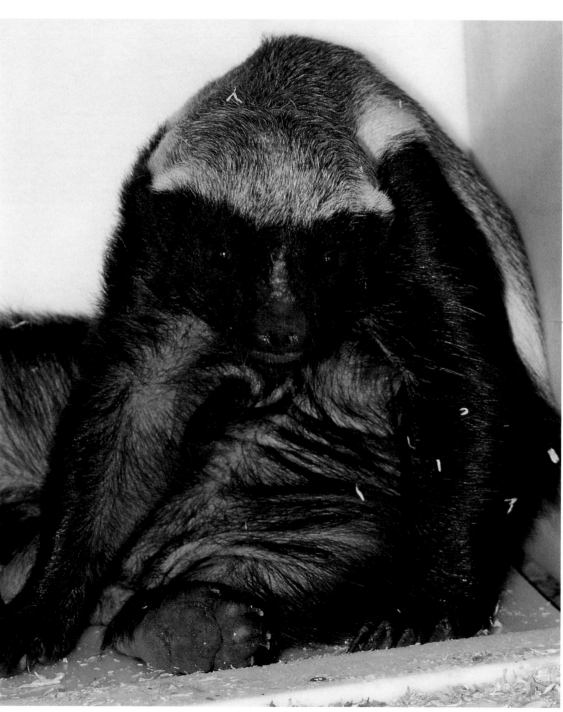

They're cuter when they're young. One of the Zoo's Vernay's ratels (right) and its offspring (above).

Shhhh!

Extremely rare in the wild, the appropriately named golden-bellied mangabeys *Cercocebus agilis chrysogaster* are only found in the southern and central forests of the Democratic Republic of Congo. These handsome primates are close relatives of guenons, and, based on their large canines, you might not suspect that they are vegetarians, which they are. They're even equipped with special cheek pouches to carry their food—fruit, seeds, insects, leaves, grass, and mushrooms. Since mangabeys don't handle stress or noisy crowds well, the magnificent primates live in a plant-shaded enclosure off the beaten path near the east entrance of Scripps Aviary. So if you pay them a visit, please observe them quietly, and if you have children with you, encourage them not to run or yell around the mangabeys.

Friendly Forest Dwellers

Like most primates, guenons are territorial. But the 20-plus species of these monkeys are fairly laid-back about it. In fact, different species of guenons, including the L'Hoest's *Cercopithecus lhoesti* (above) and the Wolf's *Cercopithecus w. wolfi*, will actually travel together in the wild, and even hang out with non-guenons, like colobus monkeys.

Singing in the Trees

Skilled at swinging through the branches, Southeast Asia's siamangs
Hylobatides syndactylus **are good at singing in the branches as well.**
You should have no problems hearing the siamangs when they're in
a musical mood. Because of their expandable throat sacs, these large
gibbons' wooing and warning calls resonate throughout the Zoo.

Pick a Peck of Pacaranas

Although pacaranas *Dinomys branickii* **have a genus name that**
means "terrible mouse," these nocturnal vegetarians are actually
slow-moving, peaceful, and good-natured. When one of these
cute 30-pound rodents is cornered by an ocelot or a coati in the
wilds of South America, however, it suddenly becomes clear
where the "terrible" part of their name comes from. The Zoo's
pacaranas will soon be moving next to the kiwis.

Of Stranglers, Shade Trees, and Religious Icons

In addition to being great shade trees with fascinating roots, the Zoo's many species of ficus provide 2.5 tons of animal browse each month. The *Ficus* genus has many notable members, including the **Bo tree** *Ficus religiosa* that shaded **Buddha**, and the huge **Moreton Bay figs** *Ficus macrophylla* and *Ficus watkinsiana* that are so popular with visitors in the Zoo and Balboa Park. In nature, about half of the *Ficus* species are "strangler figs," which grow around trees and smother them, so that the core of the ficus becomes hollow when the host dies and rots away. Stranglers don't just pick on small saplings. Our horticulture manager has seen New Guinea strangler figs with hollows as large as 10 feet!

The huge *Ficus watkinsiana* behind Flamingo Lagoon is the largest member of its species in the U.S.

International star: When Zoo veterinarians discovered that Karen had a hole in her heart due to atrial septal defect (a fairly common problem in human babies as well), a whole group of local cardiologists and anesthesiologists volunteered their time to do open-heart surgery on the Sumatran orangutan so that she could live to adulthood. The 1994 operation went well, and the sweet young orangutan became an international media star, as well as a favorite of Zoo visitors.

Like most mammals, young orangs are much more active than their parents. In the wild, they usually stay with their mothers until they're about eight.

Daydreamers

Orangutans are the loners and the daydreamers of the great apes. While chimps, bonobos, and gorillas are usually found in troops—socializing, foraging, or manipulating their environment—orangutans tend to be more solitary. It's not that they don't do all the things the other apes do, it's just that they seem to have a more internal approach to problem solving. While other apes might search diligently to find fruit, an orang will just as diligently contemplate the jungle canopy until the location of the hidden fruit seems to mysteriously reveal itself, and then swing over for its meal. Orangs have even been known to watch villagers navigate the local waterway, and then nonchalantly untie a boat and ride it across the river on their own. Primatologists are fond of illustrating the orangutan's unique approach to problem solving with examples such as this: If given a hexagonal peg and several different holes to put it into, a chimp will immediately begin trying to shove the peg in various holes at various angles, until it successfully puts the peg in the hexagonal hole. An orangutan, on the other hand, will stare dreamily off into space, perhaps scratching itself with the peg, and then, when the observing primatologist has almost nodded off in boredom, will offhandedly stick the peg into the appropriate hole, and continue staring off dreamily. Unfortunately, these highly intelligent apes are now extinct in much of Asia, and can only be found in small numbers in Sumatra *(Pongo pygmaeus abelii)* and Borneo *(Pongo p. pygmaeus).*

Take a Walk Through Paradise

The Owens Rain Forest Aviary's lush flora and fantastical fauna from Southeast Asia and the Malay Archipelago make for a delightful walk. The aviary is home to more than 200 avian inhabitants, plus quite a few fish, which live in the pool near the top. There, if you're lucky, you'll see one of the archer fish *Toxotes jaculator* squirting a stream of water to capture a gnat, or a white-breasted kingfisher *Halcyon smyrnensis fusca* plunging into the pool for its supper. In the treetops, look for the magnificent iridescent long-tailed broadbills *Psarisomus d. dalhousiae* flying by, and scan the tree trunks for the snazzy yellow crests of the greater yellow-naped woodpeckers *Picus flavinucha pierrei* (which you can also see pecking away up close in the Australasia exhibit). A bit lower in the aviary, you may notice a pair of colorful Mount Goliath lories *Charmosyna papou goliathina* sipping nectar from the silk floss tree blossoms. And at the very bottom, be sure to check out the lily pads. At first, it might appear as though the 8-to-10-inch-tall, white-headed bird you see is walking on water. But a closer look will reveal that the comb-crested jacana *Irediparra gallinacea* is actually walking on lily pads and other aquatic vegetation with its incredibly long toes. Also called lily trotters, jacanas are one of the few polyandrous birds—the female mates with several different males. In the wild, the female claims large tracts of lake and pond area, and attracts as many as three males, each of which builds a nest in her domain. She spends a few days with each male, lays eggs in his nest, and then may never see him again. She does, however, keep watch over her territory, driving off intruders while the males incubate the eggs.

Exotic, rare birds like Bali mynahs *Leucopsar rothschildi* (above) and black and crimson orioles *Oriolis c. cruentus* make walking through the Owens Rain Forest Aviary a delight. If you're lucky, you'll even see a kingfisher diving for its dinner.

White-breasted kingfisher

Greater yellow-naped woodpecker

Long-tailed broadbills have the aviary's longest nests. In the wild, predators often mistake their plant-fiber-and-spider-web homes for a trail of debris.

Spine-studded beauties: Lories and other nectar-feeders enjoy the blossoms of the floss silk trees *Chorisia speciosa* in Owens Rain Forest Aviary and other places throughout the Zoo. Even when they're not in bloom, these unique South American trees are easy to recognize because of their spine-studded light green trunks.

Kenneth Fink

Avian role reversal: The comb-crested jacana female mates with several males, then leaves her eggs in care of the males while she guards the territory.

Honey Bear Haven

Downhill to the north of Owens Rain Forest Aviary, the Southeast Asian bioclime continues in Sun Bear Forest. The 1.5-acre exhibit includes cascading waterfalls, bubbling streams, thousands of exotic plants, and, of course, sun bears, as well as macaques, binturongs, and douc langurs.

The sun bear's long tongue is good for slurping up termites, honey, and other delectable delights.

Honey of a bear: In Thailand, they're called "dog bears" because of their size and stocky, dog-like appearance. They're also called "honey bears" in honor of their favorite food. But the most common name for these intelligent, curious animals is sun bear *Helarctos malayanus*, because of their golden chest markings that look like rising suns. The smallest of the world's bear species, the endangered bears are found in the tree tops of tropical rain forests in Indochina, Borneo, Malaysia, and Burma.

Those Tolerant Binturongs!

Bornean binturongs *Arctictis binturong pencillatus* and India's endangered lion-tailed macaques *Macaca silenus* are both forest dwellers, and they both share an exhibit in Sun Bear Forest. The fact that the macaques are smaller than their omnivorous, six-foot-long (counting the tail) roommates doesn't present a problem, though, because in the wild binturongs eat insects, fish, birds, fruit, and small mammals—nothing as large as a lion-tailed macaque. Furthermore, the macaques are big and aggressive enough to defend themselves, and they are active during the day, when the nocturnal binturongs are asleep. In spite of occasional mischief from a young macaque tugging the tail of a sleeping binturong, the two species get along just fine— probably because of the binturongs' tolerant good nature. You can also see the affable binturongs in some of the Zoo's educational programs.

Short Life for a Cool Palm

You can see from its leaves why they call this a
fishtail palm. But leaves aren't the only thing that
make the *Caryota urens* unique. Near the end of
its 25-year life, the palm grows a number of male
and female flower spikes that are 15 to 25 feet
long and take two years to flower and fruit. Then
the palm slowly dies and new plants spring up
from the germinating fruit seeds. If you should
happen to see some of the seeds, however, don't
put them in your pocket. They're coated with
oxalic acid crystals that burn! The palms can be
seen many places in the Zoo, including Sun Bear
Forest and Wings of Australasia.

A Safe Haven

In spite of the fact that douc (pronounced "duke") langurs are highly endangered and only survive in small numbers in the forests of Indochina, the strikingly beautiful monkeys are still actively collected for the Asian pet trade and hunted for use as food and folk remedies. On top of that, their forest habitat is increasingly being cut down. The Zoo has helped fund a conservation center south of Hanoi that rescues douc langurs and other endangered primates, but saving this species is an uphill battle. That's why the safe haven the Zoo offers its northern douc langurs *Pygathrix n. nemaeus* is critical to their long-term survival.

Shake, Rattle, and Spike

Rattlesnakes aren't the only animals that rattle. On the rare occasions that their keepers need to crate them for an exam, Pins and Needles, the Zoo's mother and daughter northern crested porcupines *Hystrix c. cristata*, shake their tails of hollow quills to make a threatening rattle, erect their spines, stamp their hind feet, and grunt. At that point, the keepers get out of the way! In the wild, when these large African rodents feel that their life is in danger, they turn backwards or sideways and charge whatever they feel is threatening them—even if it's a lion or a leopard—slamming their erect quills into the unfortunate animal's skin!

Regal and Rare

The four raptor species in the Birds of Prey exhibit are notable for their keen eyesight, their flying skill, and their unique hunting abilities. The Zoo has high hopes for each of these rare pairs, which the Andean condors and harpy eagles are already fulfilling: They have not only hatched a number of chicks, but also have had some of their young reintroduced to the wild.

Bone Cracker

The lammergeier or bearded vulture *Gypaetus barbatus aureus* actually prefers bones to meat. Since no bird, lammergeier included, has a beak strong enough to break large bones, the lammergeiers have developed another strategy. They carry bones high in the air and then drop them on rocks, often many times, until the bone breaks. Then the vultures swallow the marrow-rich splinters and digest them with their powerful stomach acids. The Zoo was entrusted with a breeding pair of these rare birds because of its success with harpy eagles and condors. It is the only U.S. zoo involved in a captive breeding program that reintroduces the vultures to the wilds of Southern Europe.

Fisher Extraordinaire

Close relatives of the bald eagle, Steller's sea eagles *Haliaeetus p. pelagicus* are a magnificent sight along the shorelines of northeast Siberia, building their massive nests and snagging fish for dinner. Unfortunately, these birds are becoming increasingly rare. That's why the Zoo is hopeful that its almost-mature pair will soon be producing chicks.

They Leave the Scouting to Turkey Vultures

In the wild, Andean condors *Vultur gryphus* are often the last to arrive at the carrion. But that doesn't mean they go hungry. The huge birds rely on turkey vultures, with their keen sense of sight and smell, to find dead animals. Then the condors arrive and shoulder away their smaller counterparts to feast on the carcass. One of the Zoo's greatest reproduction and reintroduction success stories, Andean condors helped curators and keepers learn techniques that enabled them to save their even more endangered cousins, the California condors, from the brink of extinction.

Like all raptors, these harpy eagles are devoted parents. Raising young birds takes more work in the avian world because females don't have a built-in supply of milk with which to feed their young. It usually requires the partnership of both parents if the chick is to survive. Which is why monogamy is more common among birds than mammals.

Back Home in Panama   Harpy eagles *Harpia harpyja* have been reported snagging sloths the size of large dogs from the treetops of Central American rain forests. They're the only creatures other than humans that have succeeded in preying on these sluggishly odd mammals. Which would make you think that these skillful hunters would have no trouble staying alive. They didn't used to. Then humans came along and hunted them until they nearly disappeared from certain areas in their range. Now, thanks to laws that protect them, captive breeding programs like the Zoo's, and reintroduction programs like the Peregrine Fund's, these birds are beginning to make a comeback in the forests of Panama.

Because harpys only rear one chick at a time, when the Zoo's pair lays two eggs, the second egg is removed, incubated, hatched, and hand-raised with the help of a harpy puppet, to make sure the chick survives.

Summer in the Arctic Tundra

A harsh, starkly beautiful sweep of ocean, ice, and tundra, the Arctic isn't a specific plot of land. It's defined by an imaginary circle around the North Pole at a latitude of 66½ degrees. One of the coldest regions on earth, it is also one of the driest. With less than 10 inches of rain and snow each year, the Arctic gets less precipitation than many deserts. The king of this unique ecosystem is the polar bear—a fierce, intelligent hunter that can stalk its prey on land, ice, and sea, even if it means swimming for hours or simply waiting. In the wild, the bears have been observed sitting motionless by a seal's breathing hole for up to 14 hours. They've also been known to break into a seal's den using a block of ice, and have even been observed using rocks to spring poacher's traps in order to eat the bait. While polar bears *Ursus maritimus* make up the centerpiece of Polar Bear Plunge—the Zoo's Arctic bioclime exhibit—there are other important inhabitants as well. Such as reindeer. In contrast to the dangerous polar bears, reindeer *Rangifer tarandus sibiricus* have been domesticated by the Lapps of Finland since about 700 B.C. The Lapps not only use reindeer to pull their sleighs, but also for food, clothing, and milk (reindeer milk has four times as much butterfat as cow's milk—a bonus in such cold climes). There are also sleek and beautiful Siberian yellow-throated martens *Martes flavigula aterrima* in the exhibit, and, of course, a plethora of bird life, including diving ducks and the fantastically crested Siberian hoopoes.

Dive Right In! People often exclaim with delight when they see a polar bear loping to the edge of the water and screeching to a halt as it rises up to plunge in head first. The sight is magnificent, comical, and awesome, all at once. The best time to see Polar Bear Plunge's bears diving and swimming is just after the Zoo opens each morning. They come out from their bedrooms at a run, excited to begin swimming in their 130,000-gallon pool, and also looking for new surprises their keepers have hidden throughout the enclosure. One day, it may be 200 live minnows to catch in the water. Another day, it might be liver treats or herring-flavored cat chow hidden in nooks and crannies, and blocks of ice with treats frozen inside floating in the water. The stinkier and smellier the treats, the better the bears like them! In addition to sniffing out surprises, the bears enjoy doing full body dives, wrestling each other, and generally just having a good time. The feisty 450-to-500-pound females don't seem the least bit intimidated by males twice their size—they often initiate the wrestling matches. While polar bears are great fun to watch, when you see their huge claws splay out as they dive, or notice their giant canines gleaming as they playfully nip at each other, you can't help but be thankful there's a 5-inch-thick window between you and them. As unwary ducks that fly into their enclosure quickly find out, polar bears are master predators!

Quite a rack: Unlike many deer, both male and female reindeer have antlers, which they grow and shed every year. Males use them for fighting, and their antlers can reach lengths of up to 50 inches—about twice as long as the female's. The sturdy animals are excellent long-distance travelers. In the wild, they migrate up to 600 miles each year—summering on the tundra and wintering in timber forests.

Almost three times the size of their mink and weasel cousins, these gorgeous yellow-throated martens are capable of bringing down prey as large as musk deer.

Ducking Underwater

Some of the most popular animals in Polar Bear Plunge are not big and white. They're not even furry. They're the diving ducks, and you can find them by looking for a crowd of people in front of the aviary with the chilled pond and underwater viewing window. Unlike puffins, Arctic ducks such as this bufflehead *Bucephala albeola* use their feet, not their wings, to propel themselves underwater.

Birds with an attitude

Siberian hoopoes *Upupa epops saturata* are not only known for their spiky crests, but also for their extra-feisty hatchlings. Young hoopoes may look like helpless down-covered chicks, but any predator that sticks its nose in the hoopoes' nest hole quickly finds out differently. The chicks hiss, spray excreta, poke with their bills, strike with their wings, and launch stinky spray from their preen glands!

While eiders swim down to root for mollusks, sea urchins, and vegetation, smews *Mergus albellus* are mergansers—fish-eating ducks. Their slim, streamlined bodies enable them to swim rapidly underwater in pursuit of fish, and the tiny notches (like saws) on their bills help them catch and hold their slippery prey.

Ever wonder where those soft eider down jackets and sleeping bags get their filling? It's not from this king eider *Somateria spectabilis* (right), but from its cousin, the American common eider *Somateria mollissima dresseri*. The down is collected from eider nests after their chicks hatch.

Hua Mei and the Race to Save the Giant Panda

On August 21, 1999, Hua Mei made her appearance at the San Diego Zoo. She was the first giant panda *Ailuropoda melanoleuca* born in the Western Hemisphere in almost a decade, and there wasn't a dry eye in the room where the Zoo's panda team watched the new mom and her tiny, barely-visible baby by means of a remote camera in the pandas' den. There are less than 1,000 giant pandas left in the wild, so every birth counts. And if it had been left to nature, Hua Mei would never have been born, and her father, Shi Shi, wouldn't be alive today.

That's because Shi Shi had been mortally wounded from a panda territorial fight in the wild. Forestry workers brought the dying panda to China's Wolong Giant Panda Research Center, where he was pumped full of intravenous fluids, and literally stitched back together again. It took many months for him to recover, and he lost interest in everything but eating and sleeping. So when the Zoo received Bai Yun, a captive-raised female, and Shi Shi in 1996, the staff knew there would be more than the usual breeding challenges. Especially since Shi Shi's Chinese keepers enjoyed making jokes about his total lack of interest in female pandas.

Roly-poly and playful: At 6 months, Hua Mei was regularly climbing and exploring outdoors.

Once the pandas were introduced to their new homes in San Diego, Bai Yun quickly adjusted and began typical female panda behavior. She explored, climbed, ate bamboo, and generally did what wild female pandas have been observed doing. Shi Shi's behavior, however, was less encouraging. His long convalescence had left him with almost no muscle tone, and he wouldn't even climb a stump, much less stand on his head to mark his territory like a wild panda male. His keepers put Shi Shi on an "exercise regime." Each day, they placed his food a little higher, until he finally began climbing again.

By April 1997, Bai Yun was beginning to show signs that she was in heat. She became highly interested in Shi Shi—chirping, putting her tail up, and leaving scent marks around his enclosure. When the two pandas were put together, however, Shi Shi spurned Bai Yun's advances. When the next April rolled around in 1998 and Shi Shi still showed no interest, the Zoo decided to try artificial insemination. It didn't work that year, but it did in 1999. This wasn't just luck. A whole team of Zoo and Center for Reproduction of Endangered Species (CRES) researchers had been monitoring the pandas from day one. By now, they had figured out how to tell exactly which three days of the year Bai Yun was fertile, and the best methods to ensure a successful insemination.

Four-and-a-half months after she was inseminated, Bai Yun gave birth to her first baby. She was an ideal mother—gently cradling and nursing her tiny cub and responding to its every squawk. Her excellent maternal skills were evident as the cub grew from a four-ounce, white blob to an adorable, playful, black-and-white ball of fur that became one of the most celebrated babies in the world. Hua Mei, which is Chinese for "China USA" (and can also mean "splendid beautiful"), received her name at a traditional 100-day naming ceremony, with guests that included China's ambassador to the United States.

Having this panda family at the Zoo has been an incredible boon to their species, says team leader, Dr. Don Lindburg. It has led to giant strides in the scientific knowledge about these elusive animals, increased public awareness of the panda's plight, and led to the creation of an international team with funding to aid China in improving its panda reserves and saving their disappearing habitat.

Hua Mei, of course, is blissfully unaware of the impact that her short existence has had on the world. But it is entirely possible that the public awareness and scientific knowledge gained from her life may be one of the critical keys to the long-term survival of her species.

The perfect panda mom: Bai Yun with Hua Mei.

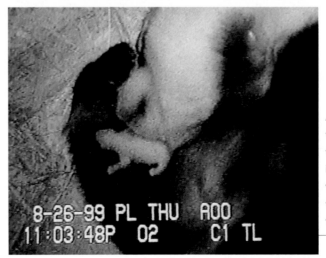

8-26-99 PL THU A00
11:03:48P 02 C1 TL

A monitor in Bai Yun's den enabled keepers to watch the progress of her new cub (the tiny white mouse-like creature that Bai Yun is nuzzling). Like most panda mothers in the wild, Bai Yun didn't leave her den for almost two weeks after Hua Mei was born—not even for food.

Hua Mei checks out the pool when mom's not looking.

Our Own Private Panda Chow

Your average American feed store doesn't stock anything that could keep a giant panda alive for very long. So, long before our celebrated pandas arrived, the Zoo planted acres of panda-appropriate bamboo, including *Phyllostachys* species like this. You can view a hillside of panda browse as you ride the speed ramp from the Panda Station up to Horn & Hoof Mesa.

Their Fur Coats Look Better on Them Than Us

In spite of their skill at adapting to varied environments, most leopards are endangered, including North Chinese leopards *Panthera pardus japonensis* (pictured) and Persian leopards *Panthera pardus saxicolor*. The reasons are common to all the cat species—they are hunted when they prey on livestock or humans, they're killed for trophies and for their gorgeous fur coats, and they die out when their habitat is destroyed and they can no longer find food.

Cats!

While Cat Canyon has all kinds of cats, it specializes in leopards. The leopards come in just about every size and color, from small clouded leopards to huge furry snow leopards—their characteristics depend on the niche in nature they've adapted to. Leopards, which are usually nocturnal, can live almost anywhere in the world—mountains, deserts, rain forests, grasslands. As long as there is enough food and cover, they can survive.

Fresh Water Cats

Excellent swimmers, Brazilian jaguars *Panthera onca palustris* prefer territories with plenty of fresh water. Unlike their close cousins the leopards, jaguars hunt more at dawn and dusk than at night. They stalk and ambush mostly peccaries and capybaras, and then drag them to a sheltered spot for feasting. But they've also been known to kill tapirs, fish, and even crocodiles.

Mountain-Top Turs

East Caucasian turs *Capra cylindricornis* prefer higher climes and navigate steep, rocky slopes with ease. Adult males usually live apart from the females and young except during breeding season, when males fight vigorously to win the favor of the females.

Drought-Resistant and Dramatic

The Pride of Madeira *Echium fastuosum* makes for a bold landscaping effect as well as providing good erosion control in water-starved Southern California. You can see the proud plants between the arch cages that are home to the small carnivores in Cat Canyon.

Legendary Leapers

Because of their speed and their legendary leaping ability that make catching small mammals and birds look easy, Turkmenistan caracals *Caracal c. michaelis* have been used to assist human hunters. Caracals sometimes raid poultry yards, however, and have therefore been killed by the people who move into the dry woodlands and savannas where the cats make their home. As for those long, black tufts on their ears—scientists think the tufts increase hearing ability and help the cats blend in with the tall grasses where they often hunt.

A Case of the Asian Blues

If you've seen the blue sheep *Pseudois nayaur szechuanensis* next to the snow leopards and thought that they didn't really look like sheep, you were correct. They're not sheep, but goats with a few sheep-like traits. Also known as bharals, the mountain-climbing bovids live in the Alpine zone of the Himalayas and China, where their slate-blue coats blend in well with the blue shale, rocks, and brown grasses of the slopes where they live.

Popular with the Hoofed Stock

As soon as they grow to a decent size, weeping wattles *Acacia saligna* are harvested to provide browse for giant elands and other hoofed stock. You can see the plants at various stages of growth in **Dog & Cat Canyon.**

What Can You Say About a Face Like This?

All right, so they're not the most attractive animals in our collection. But what these southern warthogs *Phacochoerus africanus sundevallii* lack in beauty and grace, they more than make up for in resourcefulness, strength, and intelligence. The African wild pigs forage as a family, and they are highly vocal, using squeaks, chirps, and grunts, as well as nudges and bumps, to communicate.

Ever Hear of a Mountain "Goat Antelope"?

Japanese serows *Capricornis crispus* are the most primitive goat antelopes. Though the fuzzy mountain-dwellers have an awkward gait and are not very fast, they are sure-footed and use their short, sharp, piercing horns to defend their territories against other serows, and even Asian black bears.

They Picked the Wrong Kind of Snack Food

The Indian striped hyena *Hyaena h. hyaena* hunts in a zig-zag fashion, and trots endlessly in search of carrion, its main food, or live sheep, goats, donkeys, small mammals, insects, and fruit. Because of its tendency to feast on commercial fruit, livestock, and, on rare occasions, young humans, the intelligent animal has been heavily hunted and is almost extinct in many parts of Asia and the Middle East where it formerly roamed. Hyena lovers take note: you won't be able to see the Zoo's hyenas every time you visit. The hyenas and Siberian lynx take turns being on and off exhibit in the hyena enclosure.

A Roaring Good Show

While you're exploring Cat Canyon, don't forget to attend one of Hunte Amphitheater's "Wild Ones" shows. The programs vary every day, so repeat visits are always a good idea. In between leaping leopards, a typical show might feature a male emu named Daphne showing off his amazing (for an emu) intelligence, while Salsa the coati—so named because of her "spicy" personality—demonstrates her balancing skill, and Zazu the hornbill stops by to greet you. Don't be alarmed if Zazu takes a nibble on your sunglasses during his greeting—he's very gentle.

Living fossils, the flightless emus still sport claws on their wingtips, much like those of flying prehistoric precursors such as pterodactyls.

Head trainer Kathy Marmack demonstrates one of Daphne's stubby little wings. The trainers originally thought Daphne was a female. Now they know better, but since Daphne was used to his name, they let him keep it.

Neck-Biters

The endangered clouded leopard *Neofelis n. nebulosa* (below) has traditionally been difficult to breed in captivity. But thanks to techniques used by Hunte Amphitheater's trainers, the Zoo's clouded leopards have had multiple births, and the diminutive cats that frolic in the shows are the great grandchildren of the three clouded leopards the Zoo received in 1985. The trainers' secret? They raised the three non-related cubs as if they were siblings. Because the rare Southeast Asian cats were comfortable with each other, the female didn't reject the males' overtures, which was what happened in other captive situations. Clouded leopards often reject suitors even when they are in estrus because, like most female cats, they need their ovulation induced—a painful process that happens when the spines on the male's organ tear the vaginal wall during mating. Needless to say, the females aren't going to allow just any male to "induce their ovulation." And because the female is likely to attack the male when he's trying to mate her, he bites her neck to hold her down. If she resists, he can inadvertently bite too hard and kill her. So the females are understandably wary of males they don't know and trust. Thus, the trainers' strategy proved to be beneficial for all involved, especially considering the rain forest-dwelling cats are endangered in the wild.

Big babies: Believe it are not, these snow leopards *Unica unica*, pictured with their trainers, are still cubs! The leopards' large size, luxuriant fur and other unique characteristics enable them to live in the mountains of Central Asia. They wrap their long tails around themselves for warmth when they're sleeping, and their big furry paws make it easy to navigate when there is snow.

A Lesson in Getting Along

Rocky islands that stick up in the middle of vast seas of grassland, the kopjes of Africa are a first-rate example of some of nature's unique inter-species partnerships. Mongooses scratch and sniff for insects and mice, for example, while the hornbills snatch whatever gets away. The hornbills, in turn, call out warnings when Verreaux's eagles and other birds of prey approach. Meanwhile, the mongooses gang up to kill invading puff adders, mambas, and spitting cobras. And meerkats, mongooses, and ground squirrels have all been known to share burrows at times. In the grasslands that surround the kopjes, you can find another improbable partnership—pygmy falcons and sociable weavers that share a home. You can see many of these animals in the Zoo's African Kopje exhibit.

Little Brother of the Elephant

Though most people would guess rock hyraxes *Procavia c. capensis* are rodents, the round, furry, rodent-sized creatures are really related to elephants and manatees. If you look closely you'll see why. They have pointed little "tusks" sticking out of the front of their mouths, rather than ever-growing, flat-bottomed rodent teeth. And their delightfully odd-looking feet have four hooflike nails in the front and three in the back. According to fossil records, elephants and hyraxes evolved from the same primitive hoofed ancestor about 50 million years ago. There used to be many more sizes and variations of mammals that sprang from this common ancestor, but elephants and hyraxes were the only species successful enough at filling their respective niches in nature to survive to the present.

Cliff Springers

Klipspringers *Oreotragus o. stevensoni* appear to bound effort-lessly and rapidly up and down steep rocks, even when there's no visible foothold. That's because the little cliff-springing antelopes can actually leap up and land with all four feet on a spot the size of a silver dollar! Unfortunately these unique creatures are rapidly disappearing, because Africans find their meat tasty and have many uses for their skin and fur. If they are not better protected from hunting in the few wild areas where they still survive, soon the only klipspringers left will be the small herds that live in the world's zoos.

Not Very Popular With
the Rest of the Kopje Gang
In the wild, Verreaux's eagles *Aguila verreauxii* usually chow down on rock hyraxes, but they've also been known to capture dik-diks, klipspringers, ground squirrels, mongooses, and hares.

Made to Mingle

Because they're cool-looking, prolific, and their prairie dog-like scouting behavior is fun to watch, meerkats are in several enclosures throughout the Zoo. But kopjes and the surrounding grasslands are where southwest African meerkats *Suricata suricatta hahni* **are most often found in the wild. Close relatives of the mongoose, the small carnivores are sometimes kept in African households to kill mice, rats, and insects.**

Yes, They're Really Supposed to Be There

"Look, a ground squirrel got in!" is a common exclamation from visitors who see the South African ground squirrels *Xerus inauris* mingling with the rock hyraxes and mongooses in the Kopje exhibit. While local ground squirrels have been known to infiltrate Zoo enclosures on numerous occasions, however, this is not one of them. South African ground squirrels are legitimate Kopje inhabitants. The busy rodents live in colonies like those of prairie dogs, complete with lookouts that warn them when to dive into their burrows. They feed on just about anything they can scavenge, including roots, seeds, fruits, grains, insects, small lizards, and birds' eggs.

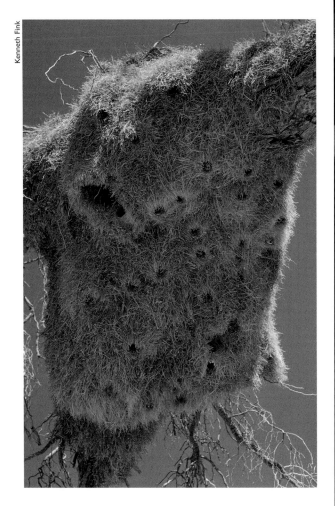

Wary Friends

Across the alley at the top of the Kopje exhibit path you can see yet another of nature's odd couples—the pygmy falcons *Polihierax semitorquatus castanotus* and the sociable weavers *Philetairus s. socius* (on either side of the meerkats). You'll know the sociable weavers because of their huge straw nest with multiple chambers—like an avian apartment building—where they all live together. In the wild, fierce African pygmy falcon couples often take over one of the weavers' "apartments." Fortunately for the weavers, pygmy falcons usually eat small reptiles and rodents. But if their preferred food is scarce, the ungrateful falcons have been known to eat one of their landlords as well. Unlike most birds that use nests strictly to rear their young, the weavers and falcons depend on the nest for survival. Since weavers and falcons die if it gets too cold, in wintertime the weavers pack in more tenants per chamber to keep each other warm, and, when they're not hunting, the falcons stay in their stolen apartment.

Pygmy falcon chicks.

Cattleya
aurantiaca

Masdevallia
rolfeana

A typical corsage orchid *Cattleya* sp.

Phalaenopsis sp.

Take an Orchid Odyssey

As Janette Gerrity, the Orchid House senior gardener, likes to put it: "You don't need to be an intrepid explorer, scaling razor-like cliffs, risking snake bites, and crossing quicksand to observe exotic orchids from almost every continent on Earth. All you need to do is make your own private orchid odyssey in the Zoo's Orchid House." (It's open on the third Friday of each month from 10 a.m. to 2 p.m.) The House, which is actually two greenhouses, is the home of 3,300 orchids from 782 species, varieties, and cultivars. Among them is the plant that gives us vanilla beans—the vanilla orchid *Vanilla planifolia*. The "beans" are actually the orchid's pollinated seed pods. You're not likely to see the vanilla orchid in bloom during your visit, however, since it only flowers one day a year. But you're sure to see hundreds of other breathtakingly beautiful flowers. The largest family of flowering plants, orchids often have bright colors to attract pollinators such as hummingbirds and insects. Some even have lips that mimic the females of certain insect species in order to lure the insect males. While you can see orchids in many places throughout the Zoo, for a truly extensive orchid odyssey, set aside the third Friday some month for a visit to the Orchid House. You'll find it on the path just west of the African Kopje's meerkats.

"Ghost Orchid"
Catasetum sp.

Wonders from Down Under

The Zoo's residents from Australia and New Zealand are, for the most part, clustered near the koalas outside Elephant Mesa. The koalas are a favorite with Zoo visitors, and the Zoo has had a long-term love affair with these adorable fuzzy marsupials, ever since the first ones arrived in 1925. Our curators and keepers have made a number of trips to Australia, to help with evaluating the status of various threatened koala populations and help with habitat protection projects and koala conservation programs. The Zoo's current Queensland koala *Phascolarctos cinereus adustus* colony numbers about 60, half of which are on loan to other zoos.

In Spring a Young Koala's Fancy Turns to Thoughts of Love
Except during their brief mating periods, koalas prefer the solitary life—hanging around in the tops of eucalyptus trees and sleeping 20 out of 24 hours, with occasional breaks to wake up and snack on leaves. In the spring, however, breeding males give up the easy life for nights of bellowing (to warn away male rivals) and climbing up and down gum trees to patrol their territory, eject rivals, and mate with receptive females.

Yawn! Raising a joey means mom doesn't always get her usual 20 hours of sleep a day.

Especially rare: The Zoo has had only two albino koalas born during its long history with the animals.

Spotted "Tigers"

Marsupial carnivores from Down Under, spotted-tailed quolls *Dasyurus m. maculatus* are also called tiger quolls. "Tiger" presumably refers to the animals' ferocity in the wild, not to their stripes, since they don't have any. With their long tails and good balance, the lithe marsupials are excellent climbers and often eat birds and nestlings in the wild. In spite of their sharp teeth and fierce reputation, Zoo keepers have found quolls to be pleasant to work with.

It May Not Be from Down Under, but with Flowers Like These, Who Cares?

Among the Australian cycads across the street from the quolls and koalas is a magnificent African tulip tree *Spathodea campanulata*. It's the one with the incredible late-summer-time blossoms.

Tasmanian Grouches

Tasmanian devils *Sarcophilus harrisii* **not only live alone, they are so unsociable that often, when they run into another devil in the wild, their ears turn red and they stand nose to nose, screeching at each other at the top of their lungs. The confrontations are usually because they both want a share of a carcass they've sniffed out—carrion is their main food. Their aggression is mostly show, however. The ornery creatures usually don't hurt one another.**

Not Extinct After All

Until a few parma wallabies *Macropus parma* **were discovered in New South Wales and a New Zealand island in the 1960s, marsupial scientists thought that this diminutive member of the kangaroo family was extinct. In spite of this happy discovery, the shy, nocturnal forest-dwellers are still highly endangered, so successful captive breeding programs like the Zoo's are an encouraging development.**

Acrobats of the Gum Tree Forest

**Across from Sydney's Grill, on your way
to Elephant Mesa, you'll find the trail to
the nocturnal Kiwi House. After you've
seen the kiwis, don't forget to look in the
enclosure to the right. You're likely to see
dozens of little creatures zipping around
and even "flying." Although they look like
mice, these feathertail gliders *Acrobates
pygmaeus* are actually marsupials, and the
females can carry up to four babies in
their tiny pouches! The little acrobats live
up to their scientific name. They have
furry membranes that stretch from their
wrists to their knees, so that they can
catch air currents as they jump and glide
from branch to branch in search of nectar,
using their feathery tails to navigate.**

A peek into a Kiwi burrow: That's dad incubating the egg.

This Is One Weird Bird Many people who see a North Island brown kiwi *Apteryx australis mantelli* aren't sure if it's a bird or a long-nosed hairy mammal. Especially since kiwis are round, about basketball size, with no tail, and well-hidden stubby little wings. They really are birds, of course, albeit odd birds. Besides having feathers that look like hair, they are nocturnal, but can't see well in the dark. They do, however, have a super sense of smell. They're the only birds with nostrils at the tip of their bills, which they use to smell and feel around for worms, insect larvae, and other tasty underground morsels. They also have sensitive feathers radiating from their necks and heads, which help them gauge information about their surroundings much like a cat's whiskers. Even though New Zealanders love their national bird, they're having a hard time protecting it. Stoats and other non-native, human-introduced animals that prey on young kiwis have multiplied throughout the island. So scientists and keepers are doing all they can to save these endangered, quirky birds. The San Diego Zoo is also doing its part, as one of the few U.S. zoos with a successful kiwi breeding program.

Oy vey, now that's laying an egg! While a chicken (which is about the same size as a kiwi) can lay an egg a day, a female kiwi's egg must grow 30 days inside her body before she lays it. Not surprisingly, kiwis have the largest eggs compared to their body size in the avian world. Hatching takes longer too. After mom lays the egg, dad incubates it for three months.

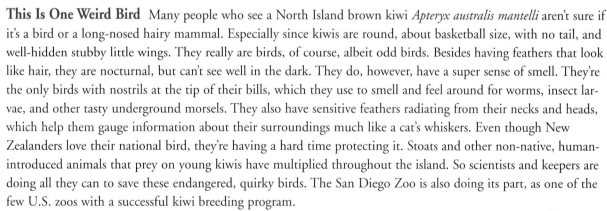

Young Sago palms *Cycas revoluta* look a bit like ferns until they mature, when they resemble palms. They are neither fern nor palm, however, but rather cone-bearing Asian cycads.

Dinner for Dinos By the time dinosaurs ruled the world, cycads were already fairly widespread, having made their appearance in the late Paleozoic. The prehistoric plants provided food for many of the giant plant-eaters and managed to adapt and survive through the world's drastic climate changes to become even more widespread today. As you walk from the north exit of Flamingo Cafe toward the koalas and down into Bear Canyon, you'll see a large collection of cycads representing each of their continents of origin: Asia, the Americas, Africa, and finally Australia.

Unlike Sagos, this Mexican cycad *Zamia furfuracea* is not likely to be mistaken for a palm because of its short trunk and leathery leaves.

Most of the African cycads, including this *Encephalartos ferox*, have hooked leaves.

There Are More Than Bears in Bear Canyon

Bear Canyon is home to the Zoo's only lions—the Transvaal lions *Panthera leo krugeri* from South Africa. So why, then, is it called Bear Canyon? Apparently, in the Zoo's early days, there were only bears there. But while exhibits change according to the needs of the animals, old names stick. Hence the King of the Beasts resides in Bear Canyon. As to where lions got the title "King of the Beasts," it's probably because they're the largest of the African cats, and because of the male's magnificent mane. This, in spite of the fact that life in a pride is fairly lioness-centric. The females work together to hunt, to raise the young, and to guard their territory, while the males play a more peripheral role.

Bear Necessities

Although Alaskan Peninsula brown bears *Ursus arctos gyas* love salmon and wolf down huge quantities of the fish when they can get it in the wild, the omnivores will eat just about anything that comes their way— grass, nuts, fruits, insects, fish, rodents, moose, elk, and dead seals and whales that have washed up on the shore. They even raid garbage cans and campers' food stashes. This bear of an appetite is one of the reasons that the Zoo posted "Do not feed the bears" signs. Some visitors were actually throwing the bears "treats" that were not only bad for them, but also discouraged the bears from more natural, healthy behaviors, such as catching the live fish in their ponds, and pursuing other tasty challenges that their keepers had prepared for them.

Oh Baby!

On January 24, 1997, the first European river otter *Lutra l. lutra* to be born in the United States made his appearance at the Zoo, to the happy surprise of the keepers. His mom and dad had arrived in 1991, and the keepers were beginning to wonder if the pair would ever get around to producing an offspring. So they followed the new little pup's progress with interest: through his first month before his eyes opened, and his second month, when his parents began teaching him to swim. Now the playful otter has grown up and moved out, and the keepers are hoping his parents will get to work on a little brother or sister. You can find the frisky pair in the waterways inside the Francois' langur enclosure, across from the entrance to Bear Canyon.

Sassy Mama

While there are only about 500 wild Bactrian camels left in the steppes of the Gobi Desert, there are thousands more of their domesticated cousins— *Camelus ferus f. bactrianus*. Just the same, Sassy, one of the Zoo's Bactrian camels, is doing her part to make sure her domesticated relatives don't become extinct. As of press time, Sassy had given birth to six calves. Her latest, Big Flynn, tipped the scales at 99 pounds. As always, Sassy was ultra-protective at first, aiming spit missiles at any keeper who dared come near her newest little darling. But when Big Flynn became less klutzy and timid, Sassy began relaxing again, and keepers could stop ducking when they came to feed and care for their charges.

Out on the Mesa

Elephant Mesa is home to more than just elephants. It has bats, rhinos, meerkats, capybaras, duikers, and even tapirs. All of the elephants at the Zoo are female, and when it comes to elephants, females take the lead. In the wild, both Asian and African elephants live in matriarchal herds of 6 to 60, with the head female in charge of leading the herd, providing discipline, and passing on knowledge. Once the herd's male offspring reach adulthood, they either roam alone or live in bachelor herds, only joining the females during mating season. The female pictured at right is a Ceylon elephant *Elephas m. maximus*.

The largest living rodents: capybaras *Hydrochaeris hydrochaeris*.

If you think bats are creepy, think again. But first take a look at the Ruwenzori mountain fruit bats *Rousettus lanosus*. With their bright eyes and cute little ears, these bats look like small foxes or dogs with wings. In fact, if you see them awake, we think you'll have to admit that they're downright adorable! Like all bats, fruit bats are an important part of their ecosystem. They cross-pollinate many kinds of plants and help disperse fruit seeds.

Not Your Typical Hippos

They only reach a maximum height of 39 inches at the shoulder, and, at first glance, pygmy hippos *Hexaprotodon liberiensis* just look like mini-hippos. But there are other differences besides size. They have rounder heads and nostrils, for one thing, and their eyes don't protrude. Their toes are more separated, with sharper nails, and they don't have as many teeth. Furthermore, they're not as social as their larger cousins—they're solitary or live in pairs—and they don't spend as much time underwater. Soon, these unique hippos will be moving to their new enclosure in the Heart of the Zoo.

Super Snouts!

Since rhinos can't see very well, they depend more on hearing and smell for environmental cues. Their tubular ears swivel around to pick up the faintest sounds, and they are super sniffers—the volume of the olfactory passages in their huge snouts exceeds that of their brains! Much of what they are sniffing to find is plant life, because rhinoceroses need a huge intake of vegetation every day. When they find something tasty, however, black rhinos *Diceros bicornis* can't use their front teeth to grab their veggies—they have none. So they use their prehensile upper lip.

Three-Toed Wonders

The Zoo has a long history with tapirs, beginning with the first Baird's tapir *Tapirus bairdii* it received as a gift from the Panamanian government in 1925. It has been successful at breeding many of these delightful animals. Which is fortunate, because, although tapirs have lived on Earth for more than 13 million years, all four of the world's tapir species are now endangered. Not only has the Zoo bred many tapirs through the years, but Zoological Society staffers have also worked on numerous projects in the wild to help protect tapirs in their native habitats.

The Other Kind of "Clouded Cat"

Though they reside on the other side of the world from the clouded leopard (see "Neck-Biters" on page 85), the endangered west Mexican margays *Leopardus wiedii glaucula* have amazingly similar habits, characteristics, and coloring. This is because, though both small cats evolved independently, their forest habitats were so similar that the process of natural selection generated copy cats, so to speak.

A Place for Galloping and Gallivanting

Bordered by Polar Bear Plunge on the west, and the Kopje meerkats on the east, Horn & Hoof Mesa contains a veritable wealth of hoofed stock, including giraffes, pigs, takins, antelopes, gazelles, and zebras. You can see several of these species interact with each other in the Veldt exhibit (below).

A Pronking We Will Go

One of the best times to visit the Zoo's gazelles is soon after their young are born each spring. That's when you'll see playful young gazelles "pronking" in circles around the adults. Pronking is a kind of stiff-legged bounce, with all four feet hitting the ground at the same time. In nature, gazelles like this Cuvier's gazelle *Gazella cuvieri* (left) use pronking for more than just youthful hijinks, however. Pronking serves as an alarm signal, it helps confuse and intimidate predators, and it lets the gazelles get a better view of what the predators are up to.

Is it Because They Like Op Art?

Zebras tend to stick together in large, noisy herds and rest together in exposed areas where they can see predators approaching from afar. It turns out that having all those stripes in one place creates a pattern that makes it difficult for predators to single out individuals. Apparently the stripes serve another purpose as well: that of group identification and socialization. Research on zebra vision shows that the animals are visually stimulated by and attracted to stripes. In fact, if you place zebras in an enclosure with striped panels in one corner, they'll hang out by the striped panels, no matter which corner you put them in. And zebras unlucky enough to be born with few or no stripes tend to be kept on their herd's periphery. The other big stripe question—is it white on black or black on white?—is easier to answer. It depends on the zebra! For these damaras *Equus quagga antiquorum*, it's black on white.

Bearded Ladies

Bornean bearded pigs *Sus b. barbatus* have equal-opportunity whiskers: both the males and the females sport bristly, white snout beards. One of the largest swine, the rare and unusual pigs can weigh as much as 700 pounds. In December 1997, the Zoo's bearded pigs gave birth to the first piglets of their species in the Western Hemisphere.

The High Life

With their stretched-out necks, their big spots, and their front legs that are longer than their rear legs, giraffes appear to be rather oddly put together. In fact, they are uniquely adapted to survive in their environment. Their large round hooves can deliver a kick strong enough to kill a lion. Their superb eyesight and hearing enable them to spot predators from afar and to communicate with each other over long distances. And, of course, their long necks and tall front legs enable them to feed on foliage beyond the reach of other African herbivores. The Zoo has had great success breeding giraffes, including this Masai *Giraffa camelopardalis tippelskirchi* mother and calf. To see a newborn giraffe emerge from its mother, spindly legs and all, and drop six feet to the ground is an unforgettable sight.

The Rarest Deer in the World

Now that they are presumed extinct in the wild, the only hope for the survival of Bactrian wapitis *Cervus elaphus bactrianus* is captive breeding programs. The San Diego Zoo was one of the first to raise the alarm and collect a group of these Asian animals before they completely disappeared. Today its growing herd is even providing mates for wapiti in other zoos. Part of this inter-zoo cooperative breeding plan involves being careful about which adult male gets to stay with which herds, and it's not just for reasons of genetic diversity. Rutting wapiti stags fight furiously for the right to be a harem's sire—roaring at each other, charging, locking antlers, and pushing and twisting until one gives up—and they often injure each other. Needless to say, this is not a safe practice for nearly extinct animals!

A Tree Full of Pharmaceuticals

Called "fever trees" because they were named before people knew that mosquitoes, not trees, caused malaria, acacias of the *xanthophloea* species are native to swampy areas of Africa where malaria is prevalent. As it turns out, rather than causing fevers, these acacias may actually have medicinal properties: African indigenous peoples have long used their yellow-colored bark for poultices to help cure breast cancer and other diseases. And now graduate students from San Diego State University are using bark, roots, and leaves from the Zoo's fever trees (some of which grow near the Veldt enclosure) to research possible breast cancer cures.

Elusive Giants

Although eastern giant eland males *Taurotragus derbianus gigas* can weigh more than a ton, they are fast on their feet and capable of majestic leaps. In spite of their huge size and impressive horns, giant elands—the largest of the spiral-horned antelopes—are not usually aggressive. They are more likely to flee than fight, and they do most of their foraging in the woodlands of Africa at night.

Put Together by Committee?

With a nose like a moose, horns like a gnu's, a body like a musk ox, and a tail like a bear's, Sichuan takins *Budorcus taxicolor tibetana* look a bit odd. All the same, many people think they're the cutest hoofed stock in the Zoo. The rare Chinese goat antelopes are a popular stop for visitors, especially in the spring, when baby takins begin wobbling around, head-butting, and frolicking. Until June 1989, when the Zoo's first baby takin made his appearance, no Sichuan takin had ever been born outside of China.

The Hunt for the Red Stag

Based on mosaics of the hunt found in the ruins of ancient Carthage and other archeological digs, we know Barbary red deer *Cervus elaphus barbarus* were widespread when the Romans ruled North Africa. At that time, they were not only hunted for sport and meat, but also used in the arena. More recent European occupations of North Africa, however, with their successive wars and hunting abuses, almost led to the extinction of these noble deer. By 1961, there were less than 50 left in the wild. But thanks to reserves that have been established in Tunisia and Algeria and captive breeding programs like the Zoo's and Wild Animal Park's, the endangered deer have experienced a welcome population increase, and now number in the low thousands worldwide.

Mighty Fine Swine

These handsome Chacoan peccaries *Catagonus wagneri* were thought to be extinct until 1972, when a researcher came across a small group in the dense, thorny forests of South America's Gran Chaco. In spite of their endangered status, the few remaining peccaries are still being hunted for their meat. So the Zoo has taken them on as a project. Not only do we have a successful breeding program here, but we also are working with other zoos to establish parks in South America to preserve a safe place for these fine swine.

It's a Cold-Blooded World!

And we mean that as a compliment. Cold-bloodedness is the uniquely efficient way that reptiles and amphibians regulate their body temperature externally. When they need to cool down, for example, they may seek shade, burrow underground, or submerge in water. And on a cool day, if they need to catch something for dinner or want to look for a mate, they may wait until midday when the sun is out. Then they will bask on a rock for awhile, until they're warm enough for the hunt. Since reptiles and amphibians don't need to keep their internal body temperature constant, they require much less food than us warm-blooded folk—30 to 50 times less! So slither and hop on over to the Reptile House and Reptile Mesa to gain a renewed appreciation for some of our cold-blooded friends.

The San Diego Zoo has had about 90 successful hatchings among its five Galápagos tortoise subspecies.

The Zoo's oldest Galápagos tortoises *Geochelone nigra* are about 100 now, but that's only middle-aged. The 500-pound creatures can live as long as 150 years.

Undoing a Man-Made Disaster For 15 million years, Galápagos tortoises roamed the once-lush volcanic islands that bear their name, 600 miles west of Ecuador. When humans first discovered the Galápagos, tens of thousands of the slow-moving giants were thriving on the islands. Within a few generations, however, the tortoise population was almost annihilated. Four of the original 15 tortoise subspecies no longer exist, and another subspecies will soon join them in extinction, because it is only represented by a single member.

How did the coming of humanity decimate a 15-million-year-old species so quickly? It was simple economics. Since the hapless tortoises could survive 18 months without food or water, buccaneers would grab thousands of them and stack them on their backs in the holds of the ships to use as fresh meat for long voyages. In the 1800s, whalers and colonists continued using the tortoises for food. And in the 1930s, turtle oil hunters not only butchered many of the remaining tortoises, but also introduced goats, donkeys, and cattle that destroyed the tortoises' habitat, and dogs, rats, and pigs that ate the tortoises' young.

Finally, in 1959, Ecuador turned the islands into a national park and passed laws making it illegal to kill the gentle giants. That same year, an international group of concerned scientists and philanthropists established the Charles Darwin Research Station on the central island to conduct research and give Ecuador conservation advice. In 1969, The Zoological Society of San Diego helped construct a new tortoise-rearing facility at the station that helps protect and restore native plant species and guards young tortoise hatchlings until they're large enough to avoid becoming prey for feral animals. The Zoo has continued to be involved in Galápagos conservation work ever since, and was even able to return a fertile male back to the island home of its ancestors.

Vacuum-Packed

Matamatas *Chelus fimbriatus* have a rather unusual method of catching their prey. The South American turtle lies in wait on the bottom of a sluggish rain forest stream. When an unsuspecting fish swims near, the matamata opens its mouth to create a suction and vacuums up its dinner!

Here There Be Dragons! While the Zoo's oldest Komodo dragon *Varanus komodoensis* is a pretty big guy, he hasn't yet grown to the size of the record holder—a 10-foot-long, 300-plus-pounder that was the world's largest living lizard. Since Komodos can live more than 50 years, though, our guy still has time to try and top that record. Found only on four small islands in Indonesia, the highly endangered dragons use their strong tails to propel them several miles through open ocean to the next island when they are looking for prey.

In the wild, young Komodos live in trees for the first few years of their lives—a wise move, because adult Komodos tend to eat any young dragons they see on the ground. Usually, however, adult Komodos feed on deer, wild pigs, monkeys, reptiles and even half-ton water buffalo, rather than their off-spring. Meanwhile, their young counterparts feast on birds, small lizards, and insects.

Sun lover: You can see gorgeous flame vines *Pyrostegia venusta* in full bloom during the fall and winter on the roof of the Komodo dragon enclosure and in the exit breezeway.

Some Enchanted Gator... Though most people think American alligators *Alligator mississippiensis* are ferocious monsters, they can actually be quite considerate—to each other, at least. Their courtship rituals, for example, are quite exciting and romantic (if you happen to be an alligator). First the male performs a kind of water dance to attract his mate, which includes creating fountains by slapping his head on the water. Then, the lovers spend several hours rubbing snouts, giving each other rides, and touching and bumping each other, bellowing excitedly all the while, until, finally, they mate. And alligator moms are known for their tender loving care. They guard their eggs for the 65-day incubation period, lunging and hissing at any intruders, and then gently carry their young hatchlings to water. There, they watch over the little nippers for up to a year, until they're large enough to fend for themselves.

A baby gator hides in the water plants, while mom and dad are out searching for dinner.

Bug Zapper Extraordinaire

It seems like it's from another planet, and it almost is. Like half of the 131 known species of chameleons, this panther chameleon *Furcifer pardalis* lives in the otherworldly paradise known as Madagascar. And like all chameleons, its unusual adaptations make it especially fascinating to watch—adaptations such as a sticky tongue that's twice as long as its body, its ability to change colors at will, its turret-like eyes that can swivel to look in two directions at once, and its pincer-like hands and feet and prehensile tail that aid it in cruising around treetops.

Getting a Grip

Geckos like this Malagasy leaf-tailed gecko (also called a flat-tailed gecko) *Uroplatus fimbriatus* can easily navigate perpendicular tree trunks in the rain forests of Madagascar, thanks to their specially adapted toes. Although they look as if they're equipped with sticky pads, the geckos' toes actually have hundreds of tiny Velcro-like ridges that can grip almost any surface, even if the gecko is upside down. The leaf-like tails of the nocturnal lizards are for camouflage, as well as a useful decoy. If a predator grabs the tail, it breaks off, enabling the gecko to escape and later grow a new tail.

Some of the most gorgeous animals in the collection, the banded iguanas look great whether you view them up close, far away, or eye-to-eye.

Unlike Zebras, He Has No Trouble Changing His Stripes

Male banded iguanas *Brachylophus fasciatus* don't need mood rings to broadcast their feelings, they simply change their color. The constant-colored bands on the back and tail of this Fiji Island resident range from blue to white, and appear to change as the lizard's body color changes from green to black. The females, on the other hand, stay brilliant green most of the time. The animals use their long tails to balance in the treetops while they're feeding on fruits, flowers, leaves, and insects. Unfortunately, their natural habitat is being destroyed by human encroachment and introduced predators, and the animals are endangered. Which is why the Zoo is involved in a captive breeding program that has produced the world's largest and most successful colony of these stunning creatures.

Of Poison Breath and Hissy Fits As the world's only venomous lizards, Gila monsters *Heloderma suspectum* and their close cousins, Mexican beaded lizards *Heloderma h. horridum*, have developed fearsome reputations. Found in the American Southwest and Mexico, the lizards have been accused of everything from spitting venom to causing instant death with their poisonous breath. None of this is true, however, though the lizards do have an impressive, wide-mouthed hiss. The Gilas and beaded lizards can only transmit venom with a direct bite, when toxin flows by capillary action into the grooves of their teeth.

Lizard breath: A Mexican beaded lizard demonstrates its impressive hiss.

The bumps are more than skin deep, as this Gila monster skull shows. Like most lizards, Gila monsters (above) smell with their tongues.

A beaded lizard hatchling.

The Runner from Down Under

Although frilled lizards *Chlamydosaurus kingii* **usually live in trees, these famous Indo-Australian reptiles often forage on the ground for insects and small lizards. There, should anything threaten them, they're known for running on their hind legs with frills extended—quite a novel sight! Because a fully erect frill makes their head appear 20 times larger than usual, it's also a nice intimidation technique.**

Water-Walker

When they're standing still, male green crested basilisks *Basiliscus plumifrons* **look like they're posing for the cover of a dragon fantasy novel. What with their spectacular crests and fanciful long claws, the Central American lizards are positively striking. Furthermore, basilisks can actually run on water! The animals (which grow to a maximum of about two-and-a-half feet) live on vegetation near water so that if danger threatens, they can either dive in or run across the water on their hind legs with astonishing bursts of speed. Our reptile curator has seen them dash across streams as wide as 30 feet in the wild! You can find the Zoo's basilisks in the anaconda's enclosure in the Reptile House. Fortunately for the basilisks, anacondas** *Eunectes m. murinus* **prefer fatter, larger prey, and the basilisks' huge roommate basically just ignores them.**

Are Two Heads Really Better Than One? Every now and then, the Zoo acquires a two-headed snake. Such snakes are the result of a rare but naturally occurring fluke that happens when something goes wrong within the developing egg. In nature, however, two-headed snakes don't survive very long—the extra head slows them down when it comes to avoiding predators and catching prey. So two-headers are fortunate to be in the Zoo, where fresh meat is literally handed to them on a platter.

The late Thelma and Louise, a two-headed corn snake *Elaphe guttata*, became an instant celebrity when she arrived at the Zoo in the early '90s. She was a guest on *The Tonight Show* with Jay Leno in 1993, and, with the help of a male corn snake, she became a mom in 1995. Then 4 feet long and 8½ years old, Thelma and Louise hatched 15 babies. As keepers predicted, all her offspring looked like dad—no two-headers in the bunch.

In nature, local king snakes *Lampropeltis getulus californiae* often include rattlesnakes as part of their diet—the venom doesn't affect them. Because of its second head, however, this king snake would have a hard time catching rattlers or even rodents for his dinner, so he's fortunate to be at the Zoo. You can see him in the Klauber buildings in Reptile Mesa.

Messenger of the Gods

The Mayans venerated neotropical rattlesnakes like this *Crotalus durissus culminatus* **as earthly representatives of gods such as Quetzalcoatl, the Feathered Serpent. The snake's periodic shedding of its skin and re-emergence in fresh, vibrant colors reinforced their belief in an endless cycle of birth and rebirth. Of the nearly 100 kinds of rattlesnakes, the neotropical rattlesnake is the most widespread. Its 13 subspecies can be found from Mexico down through northern Argentina, in environments ranging from savannas to tropical forests, and, of course, in the San Diego Zoo.**

Don't Tread on Me!

Like all the local rattlers, the largest rattler in our area—the red diamond rattlesnake *Crotalus exsul ruber*—**just wants to be left alone. If you should happen to see one while you're out hiking, don't bother it or make sudden moves toward it, and you'll be fine. These beautiful animals keep our county's rodent population under control, and getting rid of them only creates problems with the balance of nature.**

Cold Weather Python

When the light is right, the coils of the Boelen's python *Morelia boeleni* reflect a rainbow of colors. Very little is known about these extremely rare jet-black and yellow constrictors, other than that they live 10,000 feet up in the mountain jungles of north central New Guinea, where they feed on birds and small mammals.

Beautiful Dreamer

Natural couch potatoes (or should we say branch potatoes?), emerald tree boas *Corallus caninus* like to hang around on branches, snapping up the occasional bird or lizard that they find during their night hunts. Though they sleep during the day, the snakes are usually overlooked by predators because their gorgeous markings are the perfect camouflage for their spectacular surroundings in the Amazon River basin.

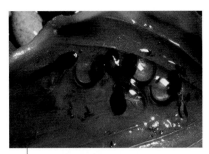

Two weeks after the poison dart female lays the eggs, her tadpoles emerge, whereupon the dutiful dad carries them to the water.

You can see the rainbow-hued poison dart frogs in the Klauber buildings of Reptile Mesa. Pictured: (top to bottom) *Dendrobates azureus* (blue), *Phyllobates bicolor* (black-legged), *Dendrobates tinctorius* (dying).

Have Frog, Will Blow Dart First let's set the record straight. Technically, they're not poison arrow frogs, they're poison dart frogs. Although a number of indigenous Latin American tribes use poison arrows, they get their poison from plants rather than frogs. Only North Colombian tribes use the *Dendrobates* and *Phyllobates* frogs' potent nerve toxins for hunting, and they use it on the tips of their blow darts. Found in rain forests of Central and South America, poison dart frogs are famous for their vibrant colors as well as their toxic skin. Less well-known, however, is the frog's unique method of reproduction. In many of the 160-plus species, the female lays a few large eggs on leaves near the water. The male then fertilizes the eggs, guards them, and keeps them wet. Then when the tadpoles hatch, he puts them on his back and carries them to the water.

Don't Eat Me, I'm Toxic!

While males and females look fairly similar in most frog species, Madagascan
tomato frogs *Dyscophus antongilii* are an exception. Even though the female
of this endangered species is bigger and more vibrantly colored than the
male, however, they're both bright enough to warn potential predators that
they're toxic. Many plants and animals have such warning signals. Red, orange,
and yellow colors are some of the most common aposematic (warning)
signs (examples: poison oak, coral snakes, bees, and fire-bellied toads), but
the "Don't mess with me!" message can also take the form of patterns, such
as the white stripes on a skunk's back.

Froggy Survival Techniques

Most frogs prefer as much humidity as possible, but that's not an option for the waxy tree frog *Phyllomedusa sauvagii*. That's because it lives in the harsh, arid Gran Chaco region of northwest Argentina and Paraguay. So, not surprisingly, the attractive amphibian has evolved several unique adaptations. It produces a waxy lipid that it rubs all over its skin to prevent dehydration. And it searches for insects by walking like a chameleon instead of hopping like a frog, using its opposable first fingers and toes to grip branches. It's also known as the Chacoan leaf-folding frog, because the females fold leaves and hold them together with sticky secretions to create a nest for their eggs. They construct the nest over any water they manage to find. Then when the eggs hatch, the tadpoles wiggle out and drop into the pool.

Just Try and Find It!

With it's mottled brown coloration and the skin folds on its back that culminate in "horns," this Asian horned frog *Megophrys montana* resembles dead dry leaves—a helpful camouflage for a creature that lives on forest floors. Unlike the pollywogs Californians are familiar with, this frog's tadpoles graze along the water surface with their large, upward-directed, umbrella-shaped mouths.

A Symbiotic Ant Farm

Near the Zoo's exit turnstiles, you can see a whistling acacia, also known as blackgall acacia *Acacia drepanolobium*. The plant's hollow galls (pictured) provide a home for certain species of ants, which, in turn, attack invading insects that are detrimental to the tree.

Come Back Again Soon!

The San Diego Zoo could not function without the support of people like you. Time is running out for many of the animals you have just seen. Exploding human populations are forcing them farther and farther back into a wilderness that is being squeezed out of existence. We might not win the battle to save all of our precious wildlife, but we must try. We hope your visit has been inspirational as well as enjoyable, and that if you are not already a member, you will consider joining us. You can find out more about the Zoo and becoming a member at www.sandiegozoo.org, or by calling (619) 231-1515.

Fine Dining at Albert's

It's only appropriate that the Zoo's full-service restaurant for fine dining is named after one of San Diego's most beloved silverbacks—Albert—who came to the Zoo as a young gorilla in 1949. Located in the Treehouse complex next to Gorilla Tropics, Albert's offers gourmet dining and includes open-air seating overlooking a private waterfall. The menu has a variety of gourmet salads, pastas, grilled meat and fresh fish entrees, as well as a full bar. In addition to its shops and restaurants, the Treehouse complex also includes a banquet room that can be reserved for private events. One of the best things about Albert's and the Treetops banquet room is that you can enjoy delicious dining with the satisfaction of knowing that all of the profits are used to benefit the work of the Zoo.

Plants

Reptiles & Amphibians

During the summer months, don't forget to visit **Nighttime Zoo**, where you'll see animals like this melanistic Brazilian jaguar *Panthera onca palustris* in a whole new light!